And the War Came

And the War Came

An Accidental Memoir

David Wyatt

The University of Wisconsin Press
Terrace Books

The University of Wisconsin Press
1930 Monroe Street
Madison, Wisconsin 53711

www.wisc.edu/wisconsinpress/
3 Henrietta Street
London WC2E 8LU, England

1   3   5   4   2

Printed in the United States of America

Lines from Charles Wright's "Via Negativa," from
A Short History of the Shadow (2002)
are reprinted by permission of Farrar Strauss and Giroux.

Lines from Gregory Orr's "Gathering the Bones Together," from
Gathering the Bones Together (1975)
are reprinted by permission of Copper Canyon Press.

Library of Congress Cataloging-in-Publication Data
Wyatt, David.
And the war came: an accidental memoir / David Wyatt.
p.   cm.
ISBN 0-299-20170-8 (cloth: alk. paper)
1. Wyatt, David, 1948– — Diaries.   2. September 11 Terrorist Attacks,
2001— Personal narratives.   3. Charlottesville (Va.) — Biography.
4. Cape Cod (Mass.) — Biography.   I. Title.
HV6432.7.W93   2004
973.931 — dc22   2004005253

Terrace Books, a division of the University of Wisconsin Press,
takes its name from the Memorial Union Terrace, located
at the University of Wisconsin–Madison. Since its inception in 1907,
the Wisconsin Union has provided a venue for students, faculty, staff,
and alumni to debate art, music, politics, and the issues of the day.
It is a place where theater, music, drama, dance, outdoor activities,
and major speakers are made available to the campus and the community.
To learn more about the Union, visit www.union.wisc.edu.

FOR LUKE

Prologue: The Good Place

The sky here is our daily bread. This evening I'm watching it from our outdoor shower as it fades from blue to pink behind the shingles of the Silver Sands. The Cape is just about the only place on the East Coast where you can watch the sun set into the ocean, as it used to do into my boyhood Pacific. Of course, I can't see the sun itself from where I'm standing, only the dune and the shrubby beach plums that hold it in place.

I soap and rinse Ann's back, turn off the water; she wraps herself in a towel and undoes the latch. I'll stand here a while, under the catalpa tree, drying myself and dressing slowly before going indoors. If I stay too long the no-see-ums will radar in and begin their relentless work.

We've had four weeks of hard-earned complacency at the cottage this summer. It's been big barbecues and peach cobblers and Cosmopolitans. I've also read some good things: *The Soul of a Chef, The Great Gatsby,*

Great Expectations, Blue Angel. Ann and I haven't enjoyed much private time, though; none for the first three weeks, when all the guests were here. I'm looking forward to an evening alone together.

The cottage represents one of those carefully tended inherited properties that give this country a patina of age and make living in it a surprise and a delight. It's one of the last buildings on Dr. Bottero Road—named, in the 1960s, after the local obstetrician—before the asphalt dead-ends into a marsh and a state beach. Ann's grandfather built it back in the 1930s, when he owned most of the lots on the street. The neighborhood was then, as it remains now, an Italian-American enclave, and the immigrants who settled it didn't believe in anything more ambitious than a cozy foothold in the sand.

So the spot we vacation in now is a slightly enlarged version of that original three-room space, where, over the decades, the screened-in porches gradually turned into rooms and the dirt basement gave way to poured concrete. The bedrooms are tiny and functional, paneled in a mysterious, shiny, and mold-defeating substance that comes in bright shades of orange, pea green, and Wedgwood blue.

The rooms of the cottage are filled with remnants of Ann's past, a procession of memories I've come to be familiar with and content to be surrounded by. Many of these are Catholic relics. Over the faux-copper bread box Ann's mother, Anita, who spent half of every day when she was alive and we were visiting vacuuming up

the endlessly incoming sand, long ago hung a repro-
duction of *The Last Supper*, painted on an oval of pine.
In the blue bedroom there is a pottery vase in the shape
of the face of the Virgin Mary. In the yellow bathroom
an out-of-body heart beats on the chest of the Savior.

The kitchen is the site of our indoor life. Rubber
tile still adorns the kitchen floor, the pine cabinets still
latch tightly, and the avocado range continues to put
out its intermittent heat. We cook and talk and play
cards around the long, Formica-topped table, backed
by the tall windows that look out onto a grassy dune.

Beyond the dune lies the beach. We actually own
thirty or so yards of it, as it is legal to do in Massachusetts, down to the high-tide line. So shallow is the
ocean floor on our arc of Cape Cod Bay that at high
tide our strip of sand is eight or nine paces wide, while
at ebb the water retreats for a quarter of a mile. Then
we can walk for hours on the gently furrowed sand, and
we spend our days following the advancing and receding tide. Some summers the motion carves out islands
that bake white in the sun, and on sunny afternoons we
lie there soaking up their heat until the last possible
moment, moving to higher and higher ground until
the lapping water sends us in toward shore.

To look back toward the cottage from the beach is
to see only sand. When Nonno Cavagioli built "the
Miami," as it was fondly called, he brought in a bull-
dozer and graded the lot flat. You could walk out the
back door and straight onto the beach. Now, after

decades of dune management and the prohibition against using anything more than a shovel as a sand-moving device, our beach grass has so successfully fixed and raised the level of the sand that we look out on dunes, on two sides of the cottage, higher than our roof. A few afternoons of every summer are devoted to clearing sand away from the foundation and wheelbar-rowing it out to the street.

In our bedroom, which faces the road, I've positioned an oval walnut table. It's there that I wrote my most recent book and where, this August, I've turned out forty pages of a memoir about growing up in Southern California. I write longhand, on white lined paper, and will type up the pages on my old Macintosh Classic when we return to our home in Charlottesville. At this point, the working title of the book is *Summer Rain*.

If I were chronicling this particular summer, I'd say that the high point was the day we took my son and my father to Provincetown. Luke grew up in his mother's house in New Jersey and has been coming to the Cape since he was eight. Dad's visit—he moved to Charlottesville from California a year ago, at the age of seventy-six—was his first. On the night I met Dad's train in Providence, a steady rain was falling. By the time we crossed the Sagamore Bridge, it was blowing a gale. I turned off the divided highway onto Route 6A, the winding post road that runs through the seventeenth-century towns of Sandwich and Yarmouth before it arrives at our turnoff, in Dennis. By then, sheets of water were obliterating my view of the center line, and we hydroplaned through a tunnel of oak and sycamores. At one of the taverns along the way, we stopped to catch our breath and comforted ourselves with a piece of blackberry pie. It wasn't until ten that we reached Gina's by the Sea, the restaurant at the turn onto Dr. Bottero Road. I knew that by now the road would be covered in water at least two feet deep.

So we parked in Gina's lot, rolled up our pants, draped towels over our heads, and forded our way the hundred yards to the cottage, through water bubbling up from the street's one sandy, clogged storm drain. We tapped on the cottage door and slid our way in, looking like two drenched Arabs and giving Luke and Ann something of a start before they began to laugh.

That was how Dad arrived. Two days later he was saying—and this is the man who bodysurfed at Main Beach well into his sixties—that ours was the most beautiful beach he had ever seen. "It is so . . . individual. There's no way to describe it except total disbelief. And yet it met the expectation. I am here in person rather than imagination. It's . . . gentle. You know nature isn't always gentle."

I'm sometimes stunned by my father's willingness to let the present erase the past. He has lost so many things that it is perhaps an adaptive habit of mind. But I know that his passion for going into water is matched only by my own and that for more than sixty years, until some big waves roughed him up, he swam in the

Pacific at every opportunity and considered living within view of it the highest privilege.

In New England, you always feel the winter, even in the deepest summer. On especially fortunate days, as the season tips toward fall, the winds blowing across the Cape drop, for an interval, and allow the clarity of the longer season to mingle with the warmth of the shorter. "Polar air," Ann likes to call it. Then the light etches the edge of every leaf. It was on a day like that that we decided to drive to Provincetown.

On the way down Cape, we stopped at Goose Hummock to price a kayak. After taking a few steps out of the car, Luke could not contain himself. "Man," he said, "this is an X-rated day. I feel like little breezes meant just for me are caressing my skin." We bought a boat and got back in the car. At Truro, we turned left onto the old bay road so as to skirt the tiny one-room beach cottages that line the shore there in such a neat and heart-breaking array. Somehow I managed to merge onto the southern end of Commercial Street, Provincetown's main drag, and as we inched our way along it, through the streams of gawking tourists, Luke and Dad, who both love architecture, began to exclaim over the widow's walks, and the trellised porches, and the tiny, overdetermined gardens that push right out to the street.

The Dancing Lobster was kind enough to seat us in a glassed-in corner with a view of the harbor. There are happy photographs of us with bibs under our chins and sauce on our faces—the restaurant's specialty is a messy-to-eat medley of Pappardelle, a whole cut-up lobster in its shell, and a spicy tomato sauce.

Afterward, we let Luke go. The last I saw of him, he was smacking a pack of Camels against his palm and setting out in search of whatever action the night might afford.

Ann and Dad and I wandered together up the middle of the street. In Provincetown it's hard to tell whether you're moving with or against the continual pedestrian throng. Dad began to prance and grin; he had already flirted successfully with the waiter and was now—for the first time since leaving California— happily inserted into the most open and relaxed gay promenade east of his beloved boardwalk in Laguna. We stopped for some fudge; Dad bought a lamp. At nine we made our rendezvous with Luke, who complained about the obvious fact that we had dropped him in a place where there were simply not any available or even many visible girls.

When I later see a photograph of this day, I'm reminded of something once said by a friend: "The three of you couldn't look less alike. There is tall, blond, angular Luke, so Scandinavian in his cool, his remoteness. You're the Slav, with the darker coloring, the flat planes in your face. And then there's your father, with that seductive smile, white-haired and blue-eyed, like a Sicilian priest."

Luke and Dad are both home now, the one in my apartment in D.C., which we share during the weeks I teach at the University of Maryland, the other in the little three-bedroom house he was lucky enough to find not a mile from the movie theater Ann opened in Charlottesville twenty-six years ago.

Dad and Luke had no trouble with the fact that most of the rituals we insist on during our month at the beach have to do with food: fried clams at Captain Frosty's, maple walnut cones at the Smuggler, lamb chops from the Dennis Public Market, gimlets on the beach at sunset. It's a place where we cook and eat and walk and read and write a little and see friends and sleep. And, once a week or so, we take in a movie.

When you marry a woman, you marry her memories, and a childhood of moviegoing at the Cape Cinema must be among the strongest and most formative of those—given Ann's eventual career choice—that linger nearby.

"There were four kids, by the time I was ten," she tells me over this evening's risotto, "Barbara, Rudy, Billy, and me. My grandfather would take us on an 'outing,' as he called it, and it was always there. We sat in those very same seats you sit in today—the unscrewed-down armchairs with the white covers. He took us to whatever he wanted to see, things like Shirley Booth in *About Mrs. Leslie* or a battle movie called *Away All Boats*. There were always large candy bars involved. Nonpareils were mostly what I had. The Cape Cinema was the 'fancy' theater, built to be part of the playhouse area. I never even noticed that the whole

thing had been disguised to look like a Congregational-
ist church."

Disguising a theater as a church turns out to make a
kind of sense, I think to myself, since my wife and I
bring to the experience of moviegoing a feeling almost
devotional. And then there's the sheer sublimity offered
up by both occasions; for my money, nothing equals
the beauty of light through celluloid except a Gothic
cathedral's stained glass windows at sundown.

"Of course there were aspects of the experience you
notice as an adult," Ann goes on to say, "that washed
over you as a child. The ceiling, for one. By the 1950s it
was a thirty-year-old building, and the mural on the
ceiling was not as crisp as it has been restored to be. I
just went inside and there was this sea on the ceiling.
Swimming creatures. Of course, it was actually the
constellations of the sky. But nobody in my family
would have heard about or cared about someone called
Rockwell Kent."

"By the time I thought of doing a movie theater of
my own, the Cape Cinema was in disrepair. The pro-
jection was terrible; the mural was almost extinct. Then
somebody from Boston came in and brought it back. I
never went on any dates there, by the way. Dates were
for the drive-in. I would never mix that up; the Cape
Cinema was where you went to *watch* a movie."

That's the memory Ann shares with me tonight.
Then we drive down Beach Street to Whig and make
the right onto Hope. The lot is full; our part of the

Cape has become a retirement zone, and the old folks have time on their hands. Besides, tonight's movie is about a late-life romance.

It's not a bad film, we agree, on our way out. The leading man and lady, both in their seventies, are still bright and smooth, with lights in their eyes. He is a widower; she's in a long, unpassionate marriage. They had been sweethearts when they were young. He writes to her, and when she responds and they have their rendezvous, they again fall in love. But the man has heart problems; we can see the end coming. Her husband discovers the affair and blows his top. One day, in a church, the man begins to play the organ, the woman begins dancing, and then she drops dead. The movie is called *Innocence*.

The man seems frail, but it's the woman who suddenly dies.

It will turn out, although we don't know it yet, that this is the last movie we will see before the world changes. The trouble with the future is that it comes before you are ready for it.

The Days

Dennis, Massachusetts
September 11, 2001

Up a little before nine this morning. Coffee and Grape-
nuts. Another clear, warm day at the Cape. We've had
more than four weeks of this weather. The phone rings.

"Have you heard?" a quavering voice asks. In the
sound coming across the wires, I can hear the quiet of
the summer breaking up. We have been *away*.

"Incoming." Isn't that one of our new euphemisms
for ordnance headed one's way? A ringing phone fills
the being before the mind can think, and to pick it
up—Ann and I have never considered Caller ID—is to
accede to who knows what kind of suddenness. I've
had a dread of its sound for thirty years, ever since the
midnight call from my father, the one that began,
"Son, your mother was killed today."

It's Barbara, Ann's cousin in Newton. "Terrorists

have bombed New York. And planes are missing. Two of them took off from Logan. Chris is on a plane out of there—I don't know if it's landed. I had to call somebody."

"Where's he headed?" Denver. As Barbara keeps talking, the door opens, and Ann is back from the market. She went out for the *New York Times*.

I turn on the TV. It's about ten in the morning. There is an image of the World Trade Center. A plane flies toward it. The plane disappears. Then I see a huge orange ball of flame, and pieces of the building falling. A voice says something about Pearl Harbor.

We won't turn off the TV today.

And we had thought of the Cape as a place where the world could not touch us.

I try to call Luke, in D.C; he caught a bus back from Hyannis a week ago. Wednesday—tomorrow—he's scheduled to begin training on an espresso machine at a coffee bar on Fourteenth Street.

It's been a long and winding road, for Luke, to that apartment. After the divorce, in 1983, his mother moved him back to her home area in New Jersey. I stayed on in Charlottesville and built a new life.

By his sixteenth year, Luke had become a guitar player and a great reader and a dedicated painter. He had also hooked up with most of the available brands of self-destruction marketed by our sad, weird America. So to have him settled, at the age of twenty-two, after the years of drugs and the dropping out of school and the car accidents and the recovery programs in the Utah desert and the Alabama woods—well, it's been a summer of great happiness and relief.

The phone doesn't seem to be working. I dial the number four times. Then Luke picks up. I tell him what I know.

What?" he says. "The Trade Center? That's insane. Those are the gates of New York. And my friend Sam works right around the corner. How did you find out?" I tell him about Barbara's call; he knows we don't watch TV during the day.

"So it's started," he says. "I'm going out with my camera." I tell him to call me later.

So it's started. It's the other shoe being dropped. We've been living high, living well, worried about the length of our vacations and the size of our 401(k)s. America is *fat*. More people than ever at the beach this summer carry too much weight.

Back to the TV. We're watching CBS. Dan Rather has a new haircut. His hair has been allowed to go gray, and his ears stick out.

Both of the towers have already been hit. The second tower hit has already fallen. The camera is on the tower still standing. Then a fountain of gray debris seems to explode upward and plume down. The building collapses inward, upon itself. The whole thing falls.

The phone rings. It's David Van Leer, calling from the Upper West Side. He and his lover, Miles, were with us for their annual visit only a few days ago.

"Have you heard?" Yes. I ask if they're all right. "Yes—sure, we're. . . ." Then the phone goes dead. The phone rings again, three more times. Each time I pick it up, it's dead.

I'm filling up with rage. I want to kick some ass; my head is ringing with phrases. I keep seeing Morgan Freeman, standing in front of the destroyed Capitol, saying "Cities fall—but they are rebuilt." I've got to get a grip; I've got to try to understand this.

I'm trying to imagine my enemy. It's important to think against myself—I think. The TV screen reads "Attack on America." They've already given this—this thing—a name. And we're all included. What could "America" have done to make itself so hated? I care about the answer, but I care more, right now, about the thought of revenge.

"Unbelievable" is the word they're using on TV. The Pentagon's been hit, there's a fourth plane down, in Pennsylvania. And maybe one near Camp David. A car bomb has been reported going off near the State Department. I've made the right turn off the Roosevelt Bridge and curved downward around onto Independence Avenue, within a few hundred yards of that building, I don't know how many times.

Dan Rather is talking to Fouad Ajami. I like Ajami; he's one of my favorite public intellectuals. It looks like he's aged since they trotted him out to explain the Arab mind during the Gulf War. I hear only a piece of what he has to say.

" . . . the Furies. They're possessed by Furies. We can't know what it feels like. There were four planes. So it takes four men. They're probably in their twenties, and all see this as a way to paradise. And they're being sent out by older men who have destroyed their countries, the poorest part of the Arab world."

Orrin Hatch calls them "bastards." He's convinced it's bin Laden, again, convinced that this is *"jihad."*

I hate the fact that already we think we know who did this. Odds are that it is something out of the Middle East. And odds are that this is the beginning of our version of the Crusades.

Bush is flying around. He touches down in Louisiana, then in Nebraska. The Secret Service wants to spirit him away to Norad; his political advisers want him to return to the White House. He says something, in his statement, about passing "the test."

Suddenly I'm worried about food. No planes are flying. All tunnels and bridges to Manhattan are closed. "Can we have hamburgers?" Ann asks, when I tell her I'm going to the store.

At the Dennis Public Market I buy ground chuck, pork chops, and mild Italian sausage.

Back at the cottage, the phone rings. It's Dad, calling from Charlottesville. "I'm so glad I got you," he says. "I had to go over to the restaurant to get through—the phone at home's not working. Can you believe it, I was on the phone to your sister in Seattle when the thing came on. She just started sobbing."

It is hard to believe. Once upon a time Meleesa was Dad's dearest love. And yet it was only this summer that they began talking again, if only on the phone, after a silence of nearly twenty years.

"So how are you?" I ask him.

"I'm feeling a little isolated. I think I'll go see Ruth and Milton. They don't have any TV and have been following it on the radio."

I mention Pearl Harbor; he was in the Army Air Corps during the war.

"I'm tired of these life-changing events," he says. "With Pearl Harbor, though, at least you knew who had hit you. The strange thing is, it's such a beautiful day here."

We talk a little more; I urge him to be with people. "I love you," he tells me, just before hanging up.

I don't say "I love you" in return. Later on, I will wish that I had.

It's hard to believe that it was just last summer that Dad packed up everything he had and left California for Charlottesville after living there for more than seventy years.

For five of those seven decades he tried to make a living in about every way an artist could: as a florist, the owner of a pottery, designer of a theme park, in vacuum-form plastics, mural painting, interior decoration. During his last and longest-lived business venture, Dad manufactured acrylic flowers. He made flowers all week and then got up at three every Saturday and Sunday and queued up his van at the gates of the Orange County Swap Meet; at seven those who had lined up soonest were allowed to dash through the opening gates to stake out a likely sales spot on the huge asphalt lot.

Dad dissolved the business in 1997. There was little to sell and no one to sell it to. Then he moved back to Laguna Beach. Laguna was the place he'd migrated to, back in the early 1970s, after leaving San Bernardino, the town where I grew up. He found an apartment on Cliff Drive, just off the Coast Highway, with a pool and a view of the ocean.

The rent on Dad's apartment was thirteen hundred dollars, about five hundred dollars a month more than he netted from social security. There was no pension and no life insurance. Every few weeks Dad's boyfriend would drive down from Long Beach and take him out to dinner. Otherwise he lived simply, averaging twenty dollars a week for groceries. He began painting again in order to make ends meet. Using basic dream symbols—waterfalls, stairways, pyramids, swirls of light—Dad turned out a series of "esoteric portraits" that represented the spiritual state of a particular client. By selling one or two of these a month, for two hundred and fifty dollars each, along with the reduction in rent he received for maintaining the complex's huge flower beds, he was able to get by.

That good life—it was hard to think of it as a "retirement"—lasted almost three years. Dad got the dream of Laguna back. On our winter visits, Ann and I sat with him in the patio sun, drinking Orvieto. We walked Main Beach to where it crumpled up in a chaos of wave-worn rock. And we drove the little roads in the back country behind San Diego in what was, for me, a sort of final touching base with the California I had left twenty-five years before.

Because we knew the time was limited, knew that Dad's California days were coming to an end. He would move east sooner or later; there was nowhere else to go. He spoke to only one of his three daughters, and she was making her own hard go of it on the big island of Hawaii. His brother Bill and his two sisters still lived somewhere in southern California, but the ties there were weak. Dad got more pleasure out of a walk downtown than most people do out of a Caribbean cruise, but he owned no nest egg. There was a small insurance policy, just enough to cover funeral costs.

Dad finally did get sick, with a serious kidney infection. When, after two weeks, nobody had called and he could barely make it from the bathroom to the bed, he decided to leave. So he piled his few possessions into his Corolla and headed east. He lived with us for a few months before we helped him buy a little house across town.

Only in the past year have I known the comfort of having both my father and my son safely situated, which, for both of them, turns out to mean living alone.

For lunch I eat a fried egg sandwich and a bag of potato chips. I'm still hungry, so I heat up a day-old sweet roll. All I want is sugar and salt.

Courtenay calls. Ann's beautiful, hard-working, daughter. She has her mother's quick temper and her curly, glossy black hair. Although, lately, the auburn dye has come out, at the sign of the first, stray gray hairs. Courtenay's in the middle of it, a third-year resident at St. Vincent's Hospital in New York. We've already seen the camera image of the crowds milling about out in front of the emergency room, on Seventh Avenue.

Ann talks to her. I ask how she is.

"Not too bad. She says it's pretty calm there. She's dealing mostly with people with chest pains. 'Mom,' she said, 'anybody in that building when it came down is dead.'"

Images of people covered with ashes, their skin showing only where the surgical masks have fallen from their faces.

Luke calls back.

"It's weird here. Everybody's out in the streets, but you can't get to anything. They've got the whole Mall area blocked off. People are trying to leave the city by walking over the Fourteenth Street Bridge. But, man, I'm worried about Sam. He's somewhere up there. When this thing is over they should do something, put up a monument. They should rebuild those towers out of lead. Try to bomb *this*."

I say something about the people who did this.

"Well, we could find a little humility out of all this," Luke answers. "I mean, I can imagine the feel of America's big thumb."

As with my father, I tell him to be with people.

"I have, Dad—I just spent four hours on the street. There are people with guns all over the place, sharpshooters on the roofs. Don't worry—I'll see you, man."

It's around three in the afternoon. An interview with a brother of one of the pilots is taking place. The man flew for American Airlines. They show a photograph. He has a big flat face and a Polish name.

I've already thought a lot about the pilots. "No American pilot would fly a plane into a building," the TV experts say. "They're trained for this sort of thing, trained to accept the fact that in this kind of situation, their life is over and to ditch the plane." So the terrorists were flying the planes. When the planes hit the buildings, the pilots were presumably dead.

The pilot's brother is standing in front of a cornfield outside his house. He gives a simple statement. "I, personally, I think I'm in shock." He talks about being "aware of the tragedy that impacted our country today." The pilot, John Ogonowski, was fifty-two. My age. As a young man, he had volunteered for Vietnam and had flown there. The brother lists the kinds of planes his brother flew over the years. "Then he went to work for American Airlines. He flew for them for twenty-two years. But what he really loved was farming, open space. He fought to preserve this land right behind me. He was always happy when he had dirt on his hands and on his pants."

The reporters ask some more questions. Yes, John's wife also worked for the airlines. When someone uses the word "stewardess," the brother smiles and says "flight attendant." Did the brother ever talk about work? No—he talked about farming. What time did he leave this morning? Around six. "We have a little tradition in the family. We all live close by here. Whenever we drive by a relative's house, we honk. Well, John drove by my uncle Al's house at six this morning and gave two little beeps."

"Do you think your brother is a war hero?"

"I think my brother is a hero for lots of reasons," the brother answers.

I find myself in tears. I'm watching this simple man, in front of his cornfield, a man with no language to speak of, a man forced to come out of his house and to confront a horde of cameras, with his hair uncombed and his shirt unconsidered, a man completely at home with the heroism of everyday life. It's not rage or grief that's filling up my eyes with water; it's the sudden reminder of human *goodness,* and of the huge, terrible, beautiful country that gives men like this man the chance to lead such unaffected lives. I haven't cried like this for years.

Something is breaking loose, inside, and the pieces of the past that have dammed it all up are moving in on me, at considerable speed.

We decide to walk the dog. Then Ann takes the kayak out; I go for a swim. It's the warmest water of the summer.

When I come back from the beach, Ann has showered. "It feels like we're at war," she says. "Everything has stopped."

Inside, the TV is talking about attacks against Afghanistan.

Chris is OK; Barbara calls to say his plane was forced to land in Detroit.

Ann calls her son, Ian, in Pittsburgh. He tells her a story about the plane that crashed nearby. Word has it that the plane was probably out of fuel and that the pilot crashed it where no one would be hurt. "And the last time there was a Bush in the White House, we killed a lot of Middle Eastern people," Ian says. Of all of us, Ian has remained the most stubbornly unforgiving liberal.

It's a day of phones and TV.

"Two hundred sixty-six people on the airplanes alone are presumed to be dead." Tom Brokaw. On the evening news.

A third building—a forty-story building—has just collapsed in New York.

"The United States, at once so powerful, and so innocent, in its worldview." Brokaw again.

Innocent. Innocence. The title of last night's movie. I hate the word, at least when it's used as anything but a pejorative. Innocence is one of the most dangerous things in the world. It refuses to remember, or to connect act and consequence. It's the worst thing about us, the belief that the past doesn't add up, that everything done doesn't finally after all *count*.

It's around seven o'clock. Bush is walking across the lawn at the White House, alone. He has come back. All I remember of him from school—once I was reminded by a college friend that that *was* George Bush—is a guy sitting on the fence in the Davenport College courtyard with a beer in his hand, directing traffic.

The *Tulsa World* has just put out its first special edition since World War II.

Congressmen are singing "God Bless America" on the steps of the capitol.

The headlines in this morning's *New York Times* read "New Leaders Talk of Possible Deals to Reduce Taxes." "Scientists Urge Bigger Supply of Stem Cells." "Nuclear Booty: More Smugglers Use Asia Route." "Traced on the Internet, Teacher is Charged in '71 Jet Hijacking."

And now, the attorney general is saying that these planes were hijacked with *knives*.

Dan Rather has just told us that there are confirmed accounts that a man and a woman, forced to jump from a very high floor, went down hand in hand.

◇

Up at eight. It's still sunny here, cooler, with a stiff breeze. The first thing I hear on TV, from an Englishman, is that "the dollar is not going to collapse." Ann, as usual, is out early, walking the dog.

A woman whose son was on the plane that crashed in Pennsylvania is being interviewed. He called her on a cell phone before he died, about fifteen minutes before the end. She is certain that Mark acted, that, like another passenger also able to call out, he decided, "We're going to do something, because we're going to die either way." A Cal grad. A rugby player. Very aggressive and smart, his mother says. "The phone call in some ways has to be thought of as a gift," the interviewer says. Then the mother begins to weep.

Our first cell phone disaster. People knitting the world together, creating a vast, broken web of voices.

And here is a sample of the morning's incoming, the unbearable insistent list:

Gas in Peoria is up to four dollars a gallon.

Major League Baseball has canceled all games indefinitely. Jay Leno is off the air for a week. The Emmys are canceled.

There's a spontaneous pro-American demonstration taking place on the Unter den Linden.

The new word is "harbor." We will now go after those who *harbor*.

Israeli rescue teams are being flown to the United States, along with donated blood. Ten Palestinians were killed last night.

The Pope, sitting in his chair, said this morning that "yesterday was a dark day in our history." Putin says, "We are with you."

In New York, dogs are being sent into the rubble. No commercial planes will fly today.

It's going to be like chasing mercury with a spoon.

I drive to the market for a paper. The *Boston Globe* rack is empty. "We sold out at 6:15," the checker says. "Things were crazy."

I find the *Globe* at a box near the post office. Its headline reads "New Day of Infamy." The mystery unfolds. Some of the hijackers flew to Logan from Portland, Maine. They were armed with knives and "cutters." The *Globe* writes that "Americans must give a proper name to the horror." The paper goes on to say that if this is terrorism, it is also "war." To call it this, of course, is to then allow ourselves to suspend the rules. It's not going to be resolved by a trial, by seeking justice.

It's ten o'clock. Six survivors have been found in New York. Firefighters and a police officer.

The *New York Post* reports that grocery stores were cleaned out yesterday. "There's no water, there's no milk, no bread. This is like getting hit with four blizzards in one day."

All the talk of airport security baffles me. Isn't it now clear that we can't stop a truly determined individual from taking over a plane? I can even imagine doing it myself. Unless people enter planes unclothed, and without any baggage, who knows what sort of weapon cannot be smuggled on? I think about the end of *Godfather III,* where a man is stabbed in the neck and killed with his own glasses. It's all about the level of feeling against us. I remember the book read in college that defined a fanatic as anyone willing to act against his own interests. Meaning—any person willing to die on behalf of his crazy beliefs.

A man named Ackerman is talking about St. Vincent's Hospital. So far they've seen 365 victims. Only four have "passed away." "The sad part of it is there's just not many survivors." I wonder how Courtenay is doing. She's certainly ready for this; her specialty is critical care.

Ann and I turn off the TV and go for a bike ride. It's a brilliant day, with sharp shadows. Zinnias and cosmos in late-summer bloom. There aren't many people about: a man mowing, one jogger, two white-haired ladies taking a walk. At Corporation Beach we see perhaps twelve cars. A man in a chair on the beach sits next to a cooler; he's drinking Diet Pepsi. I think of the fall to come, the darkening of the year, and of how hard it would be to face all this with the heat of the summer still ahead of us.

The Arlington fire chief has just ordered the evacuation of the Pentagon.

Reid calls from the theater; he manages it for Ann. She opened Vinegar Hill in 1976 as a rep house—her first big hits were *Casablanca, King of Hearts,* and *The Harder They Come.* Now most of the old art houses are gone, but Ann has managed to keep hers open, in the northeast corner of Charlottesville's downtown mall.

"We closed last night," Reid says. "We'll be open today, although we haven't been doing any business anyway." This week's movie is *The Anniversary Party.* He talks about the images coming over the TV. "It's like *1984.* You're all underground, and the screen tells you that we destroyed their stuff, and that they just destroyed our stuff. Control through special effects."

"No sense of how it will end," I say.

"I don't think religious wars do end."

"Have you seen Dad?"

"Oh yeah. We just talked; he's next door, at the restaurant. He felt like washing the floors. Says he's televisioned out."

The booker for the theater, it turns out, was stranded in Toronto. He just got back by driving to New York. The news is that we will play *Hedwig and the Angry Inch* on Friday—if the print gets there.

Ann just returned from the bike ride; I cut mine short. "I feel much better. I sat at Sesuit Harbor and watched them take boats off the racks like cans of tomatoes and put them in the water."

News chatter: NATO is about to invoke, for the first time, Article 5 of its charter, which states that an attack on one member nation is an attack on all. And someone called from United Flight 93 and reported that a fight had broken out between the passengers and the hijackers. We're all combatants now, I say to Ann at lunch. No more sitting tight.

Trying to imagine what happened on that plane—that flying coffin—fills me with a flooding warmth. "Some of the male passengers . . . " Dan Rather says. "Some of the male passengers . . . a hellacious scene on that aircraft."

The government now believes that there were three to five hijackers on each plane and that at least two on each plane were pilots.

Ann and I take Norma for a walk on the beach. The tide is out. Norma has been running away and jumping up on people, boxer-style, in a friendly way but one that can be scary. We've had to keep her on a leash. Today Ann lets her run, and she finds a couple to harass. The big problem of the vacation, so far, has been an unruly dog.

We talk about a solution. Build a wall, I say. Move all the Jewish settlers out of the West Bank, back to Israel, give that land to the Palestinians, naturalize any Arab who wants to stay in Israel, and then build a wall. No coming and going across it. The idea of the multicultural state has failed.

Of course, that would take care of only half the problem. I tried to read the Koran last fall. What I read—and it wasn't much—was a series of prohibitions and lots of "Praise the Lord." The stories that it told it sometimes appropriated from the Bible, and they seemed, in their awkward retelling, to miss the point. It was as if an inattentive sophomore had handed me his lecture notes and told me, "But this is what you said." Here is where my intolerance comes out, in the insistence that a sacred text be . . . *well written*.

I wonder if cultures without adequate narratives can develop in their peoples an inner life. Yet for centuries Islam was a great and accommodating culture, a place of high thought and refuge. It harbored the Jews the Christian world cast out. *Harbored*.

I just read something interesting in Holman Jenkins's column in the *Wall Street Journal:* "An intelligence official once told me that most suicide bombers are unwilling emissaries. Family members are held hostage and threatened with torture and death to give these beloved sons added incentive to do their duty."

I call Dad. He's been napping and sounds sleepy. "The strange thing is that it's so lovely here," he says. "I woke up and felt tired, but I said to myself you're not going to get untired by sitting around. So I went over to the restaurant to do the floor and work on the flowers. The window boxes are almost obscene; I even had to stake up the marigolds. I'm trying to stay in that reality. You see, we've all had our little Armageddons, over the years, and we've done pretty well with them. That's where I want to live. I did call Lida, though, to talk about remembering the day of Pearl Harbor. But, you know, all this has gone on around me, and I've been strangely untouched by it. And at least, today, I have a clean floor."

Ann's outside, tearing down the fence along the end of the driveway. At around five we go down to the beach. Ann takes the kayak out for a long paddle; I swim up the beach a little. The water is warm and full of seaweed.

It's going to be a life of jagged transitions. Tonight we face a chore we've put off for weeks; for a few hours we will have to put the world aside. It's time to go over the books for L'avventura. That's the name we gave to the restaurant we built four years ago and are now, after many painful discussions, thinking about selling. I say something to Ann about generating "the numbers," and she knows what I mean.

"OK—but can we have a bottle of wine?"

I open a Brunello. How odd it seems, to be worrying about a world in which what matters is the amount of hot pepper in the bucatini all'Amatriciana.

The gross receipts for L'avventura turn out to look like this:

1997	$154,414
1998	$279,716
1999	$287,322
2000	$314,000

Our food costs for the last three years average 30 percent, right on the mark for any respectable restaurant.

"I think this place will look like a gold mine to a young, energetic chef," Ann says.

Why did we decide to build a restaurant? By 1996 we had clearly come to the end of something. Ann's children were grown, the theater functioned like a well-oiled machine, old friends had moved away. Al Filreis was busy raising kids in Philadelphia and computerizing Penn's English department. Bob Schultz, working away in Iowa, had published his first novel and was well into his second. David Van Leer, another professor friend, was busy shuttling between his teaching job at Davis and the Manhattan apartment he shared with Miles. If we were lucky, we saw each of them once a year, usually at or on the way to Cape Cod.

Jahan Ramazani and Barney O'Meara—my best student ever and my college roommate—remained closer to hand, within an hour's drive. But both were working so hard—Jahan at presiding over the Faculty Senate at Virginia and Barney at his technology transfer business—that we did well to grab dinner together twice a year. Happily, we had again begun seeing Greg and Trisha Orr—they have lived in Charlottesville as long as I have—and the four of us talked mostly about our children or our parents, musing together about our strange middle-aged station in time.

My teaching job at the University of Maryland provided me with my biggest dose of society, and in the year we conceived L'avventura I had four dear friends there—the poet Stanley Plumly, the film critic Bob Kolker, the novelist Howard Norman, and the James scholar John Auchard. Because of them the drive north from Charlottesville to College Park felt less like a return to work than like the resumption of a warm and witty conversation. And these men took care of me: Stanley passed along his barely worn sport coats, Howard showered me with newly minted books, John found us hotels in Milan, and Bob cooked me dinner at least once a week. But this society was available to me only midweek and did nothing to alleviate the quiet of long weekends at home.

Ann felt more lonely in her days and had begun saying things like "I do feel like my previous life has been bronzed. The seventies are just so far back there. Of course, we all had lovers then. What else was there to do in the afternoons?"

So, as we so often do, we cooked up a building project. Ann owned the land, a little trapezoid of parking lot in front of the theater lobby. We hired an architect, borrowed two hundred thousand dollars from the bank, and built right up to the city sidewalk, which accounts for the almost imperceptible dogleg in the front wall where it hugs the oblique angle of the property line.

We decided to name our place after one of our favorite Antonioni movies, to bake our own bread, to offer at least sixty wines, and to serve the simple Italian food we had eaten in little restaurants in Rome. A grilled pork chop—and nothing else. Bucatini all'Amatriciana with

32

lots of red pepper and pancetta. Risotto with mussels and saffron. Potato gnocchi with basil and ricotta.

We've had great times—evenings when the place was so full and the food so smooth that the tiny space took on the intensity and glamour of the deck of a man-of-war. Each to his station, each to his task. Any lapse of attention, and the battle is lost.

People *reveal* themselves in a restaurant, above all the customers. Tipping is a straight measure of generosity, and the old friend who carries a card in his wallet that allows him to calculate the gratuity to a precise 15 percent is someone I've stopped speaking to. Ordering food tests the spirit of adventure; wine, the distance won from our culture's abiding Puritanism. Can one sit in a booth for two hours with a partner of twenty years and make good conversation? A surprising number of our customers do, and I've come to appreciate the many solid marriages in town. But the customer, however chic, is like the student: he thinks the show is about him, but it's really about the dish being cooked or the book being read. The loyalty is to the *material*. I have nevertheless become fond of many of our regulars, people I would otherwise never see.

But, after four years of mounting personnel problems—we've had to fire a cook and a dishwasher this summer—and making just enough money to cover the bills, we have decided to sell. We made the decision before coming to the Cape, but, now—well, who knows what kind of money will be floating around?

It remains remarkable to me that we have done this thing at all. I had never run a restaurant, and Ann withdrew from her initial try at one, a marriage-saving venture with her first husband, a year after it opened. Our kitchen has a very short line with two cooks—grill and sauté—working side by side. It's tricky to work so close to your spouse in a situation where you both have strong opinions and care so much about outcomes. When she's feeling beaten down by the job, Ann speaks of her "sadness." It's an emotional burden, like so many of those we carry, handed down from childhood, the voice inside that whispers that her efforts will fail. "You were dropped on your trust," her therapist quipped one day, and it's a line we trot out and even smile over, if we're feeling companionable, when Ann's sadness returns.

We own six aperitivo glasses that we use for Amaros. A white line runs around the waist of each glass, with the word *"ottimista"* painted above the line, the word *"pessimista"* below it. Together Ann and I make a glassful.

What Ann feels about the restaurant is of course real to her, but I fight to remind her that her feelings are independent of the fact of what we have actually done. Because the place *is* a success. Not perhaps as the world defines the case; we haven't made a lot of money or garnered rave reviews. We do make food the way we think it ought to be made. On bad days, I console myself with the thought that all one can do is to offer the world one's gift.

At 9:30 the TV tells us that a *Time* magazine website is reporting that some passengers on Flight 93 were able to whisper into their cell phones the seat numbers of some of the terrorists. It is also claimed that some of the pilots among the hijackers flew for Saudi airlines.

Today I finished reading the book manuscript of a colleague up for promotion and tenure at Maryland. I'll be chairing the promotion committee, despite the fact that I'm on leave for the fall semester. Last year the English department failed to get its candidate through, so there's a lot riding on the case this year.

Courtenay just called. I hear only Ann's part of the conversation. "Oh my God. There are no bodies? So it's just going to be one masquerade? They've been taking truckloads? Your resident lounge? There aren't enough bodies? It smells like smoke and flesh. Oh God."

"All last night? What you told me yesterday at noon was what the news said at nine. So do you have relatives coming through the lounge to identify bodies? So the ER was trauma central? Right. Right. Everywhere. You were there all night? Oh. Yeah. Yeah."

"But so many of them are missing—I mean the fire-fighters. So they're saying that two hundred firefighters are dead? You think there are ten thousand people? I can't watch that, I see it in my dreams, I see it in the daytime."

"I assume that that would be the sensation, that you want to stay there. So you went home and slept all day.

Yes. Usually when I watch it I start to cry. It's just silent—silent. I guess you don't go any further south than where you are. How many doctors went down and didn't come back? Oh God."

"I'm still back with the ash and the barbecue smell. So people were actually bringing food to the hospital? Just people on the street. And now you've got restaurants bringing food? That's great. Yes, I've been amazed at the level of integrity and grace under fire. You know who looks amazing on TV? Giuliani. As opposed to the man who is our president. He looks like—'What do I do?'"

"No. None of us are going to be the same. You feel that this is a city where all the faces and all the energy are devoted to helping, helping. Whereas Luke says people in D.C. are trying to walk out across the bridges. He makes it sound like a John Carpenter movie."

They talk about the dating scene with her friends, about colleagues disappearing in the middle of the day, pursuing romance. Ann goes on. "I think that the other day, before this happened, I just realized that when I was out in the world serial dating, I was behaving like a serious person, but unless everybody understands the rules, it gets kind of messy. Sometimes serious people are appealing, but when they continue to be just serious, they're less so. Hello—hello? I think this conversation may have ended."

◇

I wake up to the news that seven hundred thousand people have called the Red Cross with offers of help. Airports will reopen on a case-by-case basis.

Ian called last night from Pittsburgh, after Ann talked to his sister. His local news is carrying a story about an unmarked plane that shot down the plane that crashed nearby. Steak knives will no longer be issued in first class.

Ann's brother Rudy is coming down today for his first visit of the summer, so I drive to the store for doughnuts and beer. In the old days he used to arrive with a case on his shoulder and work through it in a day.

The lead article in the *Times* this morning reads as follows: "The hijackers who commandeered commercial jets that attacked the World Trade Center and the Pentagon were followers of Osama bin Laden, the Islamic militant who has been blamed for some of the bloodiest attacks against Americans, federal authorities said today." The same page contains an article on 359 lost firefighters. My reading this morning yields these facts: the air force has a "policy for when a civilian plane could be shot down, but the agency would not discuss it." Five men in Union City, New Jersey, set up cameras on the day of the attack and congratulated one another after the planes hit. A man with a megaphone on the south tower's forty-fourth floor told people

"Our building is secure" and urged them, minutes before the collision, to go back to work.

The sound of this war feels as if it were reeling straight out of my mind and heart. I love the odd and suggestive use Heidegger—or perhaps it is his translator—makes of the ordinary English word "thrown." To have being in time, he argues, is to feel released into an unstoppable momentum, as a baseball feels when delivered from a pitcher's hand. To accept this, to come to savor it, is to agree that Hamlet was right when he said that the readiness is all. But there is no getting ready for what has happened and for what will go on happening to us, no way to manage the soul-bruising overload of feeling and fact or the sheer incommensurability of taking it all in while continuing to live our little lives.

I think I am right in assuming that for Heidegger there is no pitcher and there is no receiving glove—there is only the hurtling ball.

When Rudy shows up, we talk about cars. He owns a garage in downtown Milford, does some welding. Every Friday his "motorhead" friends, as he calls them, meet at the garage for beer and cold cuts. Ann was the one who left New England; Rudy was the one who stayed.

"So are you still running the social club?" I ask him.

"Yeah, what are you gonna do? I tried to clean them out earlier in the summer, but that didn't work. I'm worried about finding them in the intersection, asking 'What happened?,' wandering about like deer."

He has brought Ann's annuals from high school. I look through one in which she is pictured both as "Most Studious" and "Most Likely to Succeed." "I was the editor," she says. "I had total control."

Inside, Bush is giving his first press conference. He says something about the need "to route out and whip terrorism." Later on, he uses the word "whipping" again. "This is now the focus of my administration." When asked about his prayers, he starts to tear up. He says, "I'm a loving guy," then breaks off and quickly leaves the room.

The three of us take a walk on the beach. It turns out to be the longest walk of the summer, as we follow the ebbing tide, cross the channel, and go as far as we can toward Sandy Neck. Rudy comments that the beach is flatter and shallower than usual. At one of our stops, we talk about a terrorist cell that has been discovered in Springfield.

"They're lettin' too many people in," Rudy says. "If you're going to live here, you should know English. I've got people coming to the shop who can barely talk."

The obsession with plane security comes up. I propose that air crews be allowed to keep weapons in secret places on the plane. "But what about the cleaning people?" Rudy says. "No, it would be better to let them bring weapons on with each flight when they board and then put them in a secret place. And the pilots and copilots should be armed." We talk about the danger of a gunfight in midair, about the sense that everyone can now be seen as a soldier and faces the issue of self-sacrifice.

It's a day of listening to a brother and a sister talk about old friends, about how the marriages are playing out, whose property has been sold or neglected, cars repaired or exchanged, graves visited. Rudy is wearing his "Tri-Town Street Rods" T-shirt.

Back at the house, the news is claiming that the FBI has identified all the hijackers.

Andrew Young, asked by Tom Brokaw what the message is in all this, responds that "the message is that we shall overcome." He also says that "this is an attempted rape of civilization." We have things "well integrated" here, and some people resent that. They feel rage at our success. When Brokaw points out that he might find it surprising to now be considered an elder statesman, Young laughs. "That makes two of us. Whatever happened to Huntley and Brinkley? The giants that we looked to are gone, and, well, we've got to perform."

On TV yesterday, someone used the word "fear" to describe what Americans are feeling. I scoffed at the word. It's certainly not what I feel. I have to admit that the odds of myself or of someone I love being hurt by terrorists are very small. I suppose I rely on the probabilities. My apprehension is over how this will change us and the way we live. The years since World War II will come to be seen, I am beginning to believe—even counting the upheavals of the 1960s and maybe even the nuclear dread of the cold war, although about this I'm not sure—as the Great Good Time. We built a country. We moved about freely. We opened our borders and stirred the pot. The possibility of going to college and of becoming a university professor—surely the most privileged of professions—became a reality for millions. We learned to live so well that we even began to worry about the quality of our food. "But that's the way we *should* live," Dad said yesterday, on the phone, when I referred to being caught up in some small piece of dailiness. We *are* safe here. The other night, Ann remarked, almost as if in self-reproach, "I feel like Ava Gardner in *On the Beach*. So far from things."

It's our last warm day at the Cape; a cold front is blowing in. Cloudless, with a light breeze. I've taken a little nap, walked out for a dip. I'm inside now. I'll make martinis, grab a beer for Rudy, and climb over the dune for the sunset. I will not turn on the TV.

On the beach, we talk with Rudy about a diner he's been trying to save. "The town wouldn't help us at all. The diner didn't have a back wall—it was attached to a house—and we wanted to move it next to the garage for a sort of clubhouse." We talk about Milford's downtown. It's dying; all the shopping has moved to the rim. "Downtown's full of Brazilians and Cape Verdeans." Ann guesses it's the Portuguese connection. "Maybe. But you should see the welding some of these guys do. You wouldn't believe it." I say something about needing

German engineering. "Yeah, I know what you mean. I've got this friend who is German. I think he's Jewish. He's so cheap, he squeaks. And he's so smart, it's depressing."

Ninety-one percent of Americans, according to an NBC poll, see the attack as equal in seriousness to Pearl Harbor.

Luke just called. I ask him about the job. "Yeah, I did training yesterday. Just watched. I didn't realize that I already had the job. I'm being trained by this little Peruvian lesbian—she's real nice. I don't quite get how to make foam, though."

I ask about the mood of the city.

"Nothing is happening here. It's totally quiet. There's a neighborhood feeling, people in the parks. I think something has kicked in for Bush, though. This thing has given him a focus. Clearly he can't talk, but he seems psyched up. And thanks for the mail, by the way; it came just in time. I was down to two dollars. I've got to run—I'm going to hook up with a guy I met and go to a show."

After a dinner of pork chops, we share some grilled plums. "You're spoiling me," Rudy says. He's a lifelong bachelor, although he lived with Anita, Ann's mother, until she died a few years ago. Now he's talking about staying regular. "Just eat some raw garlic or onion. Then a Nature Valley granola bar. Next day, man— wow!" He talks about getting married. "But I like my life. I can walk around naked when I go upstairs. Burp. It's beautiful."

"You can do that with somebody, too," Ann responds.

◇

Dennis, Massachusetts
September 14, 2001

It rained hard last night in New York, creating what reporters are calling an "oatmeal-like mud." Here it's cloudy and windy, with no rain yet. I'm out at seven to walk the dog.

Logan and all New York airports are still closed. Reports claim that the planning of Tuesday's events may have been in the works since 1996. The *Wall Street Journal* writes that opening some airports while keeping others closed is a recipe for disaster. The airlines have only fifteen days of cash reserves. The *Journal* suggests that crews be issued pepper spray and that the cockpit never be opened after takeoff.

I'm drawn to a story about Jeff Bezos, of Amazon .com, perhaps because our friend Ellen—the woman who introduced us in 1982—works for the outfit as a web designer. Stranded in Minneapolis, Bezos rented a Mazda minivan big enough for his team of five. They bought fresh T-shirts and underwear at Marshall Field, stocked up on food at Burger King, and then hit the road for Seattle. They also brought along compact discs by Bob Seeger and Steve Miller.

A phone call from Iowa. It's Bob Schultz, a fellow English professor and an old friend. It's been a month since he and Sally were here for their visit. We alternate the site of our annual reunion; one year it's Decorah, one year it's the Cape.

He talks with Ann, then she hands me the phone. "I saw that slow-motion video," he says, "the one where the second plane goes in like a hypodermic, and a phrase flashed into my head. 'Reckoning Angel.' There's a sense, somehow, that we've called this down on ourselves." Thoughts, I answer, I've also had. "But there's no excusing those—" he gropes for a word—"those insane murderers. We should be hunting them down like dogs."

We talk about the parts of our culture that offend us, and yet how much we think about revenge. "What in our culture are we ashamed of—ourselves—in this moment of high seriousness?" he wonders. "We've been attacked in the most monstrous way, and yet it's like the kind of movies we make. It feels as if we imagined it and then it happened: There's a lot to sort through— deep complications—but we're not going to have that luxury."

We talk about work. Bob is the new chair of his department this fall. "I have been extremely busy this semester. Worked until eleven on a promotion letter last night. Sally gets up, goes to work, I get up, go to work, she comes home, we have dinner, I work, she goes to bed, later I go to bed. She says she can't listen to Bush—he talks like a high school kid. So reflexive."

"No," I answer, "he's not in his language—not yet, at least."

"When I had to go back into class the day after, I didn't know what to say. We were supposed to cover the last four books of the *Odyssey*. A freshman class—their first month away from home and this happens. I told them I knew we all had terrible images in the backs of our minds, that something important and preoccupying had happened, that it probably seemed like talking about an old book was trivial. I told them straight out that I didn't know what to do. The only thing I was sure of, I said, is that this was going to test all of us, that it would be a complicated thing to think and feel our way through. I told them I believed in the kind of education they were starting, that feeling their way through a big, subtle book was training for their sensibilities. The only thing I could think to do was to go ahead with it. They seemed relieved. Later in the hour, somebody noticed that Athena had to step in to stop revenge from consuming everyone."

We talk about our families. Bob and Sally are going to eat at the hotel where Schuyler is cooking the special. A senior at Luther, he's thinking about cooking school after graduation. "He told me he spent four hours in bed listening to NPR," Bob says. "He said he feels like the only thing he can do is pay attention."

Today we will clean up the cottage before leaving tomorrow; Rudy helped us carry the kayak into the basement before he took off this morning. We unscrew the awnings, put away the Adirondack chair, sweep and vacuum, do laundry. I'm grateful for the work. Afterward, we have a lunch of poached eggs.

"He looks better than he ever has," Ann says about Bill Clinton, as we watch him wiping his eyes while talking to a man in a skull cap after today's memorial service in Washington.

"He's free," I say. There goes Al Gore, in his new beard.

Amtrak ridership is up 60 percent; Coca-Cola has halted all U.S. advertising "out of respect" for the victims and the rescue effort.

The FBI is releasing the names of the hijackers, now numbered at nineteen. Some have been living for years in Florida and California. The names go up; they are all "Arab" names. No photographs are yet being released. Two of the hijackers may have attended U.S. military schools.

Ann just came back from the dump. "I can barely drive the car. I was just undone by all the flags. There are little flags on the lawns, big flags on the houses. Even some with the stars in circles. It's too much—just too much."

Powell is giving a press conference. It's the most reassuring performance I've seen yet by a federal official. When asked if he has a message for the Taliban, he answers, "To the extent that you are providing havens to organizations such as Osama bin Laden's that is attacking civilization and killing innocent people . . . you cannot separate your activities from the activities of the perpetrators."

The House has voted 422 to nothing to appropriate $40 billion to the rescue and war effort.

It's raining again in New York.

The FBI has four thousand special agents working on the case. They have already received thirty-six thousand leads. Most of these have come over the Internet. At this moment, they are questioning the director on TV. Someone has asked a question about a District police bulletin regarding a silver minivan carrying a chemical weapon. Luke is in the city. I think about that. I think that if something happened to Luke, I would do *anything*.

Ann and I take a walk down the block and back into the little sandy roads like Wade's Way and O.K. Avenue. No one about. On a trail to the beach, there is a heavy, sweet smell. Wild grapes.

Bush did much better today, at the National Cathedral. "The commitment of our fathers is now the calling of our time." He is in New York now, touring the wreckage. Over the bullhorn he says, when the crowd protests that it can't hear him, "I can hear *you*. And the rest of the world hears you. And the people who knocked these buildings down will hear from all of us soon." I like the sound of that.

47

New York airports have reopened. Massport has decided to reopen Logan tomorrow.

Downstairs Ann found the flag that was used for her father's funeral—he was a veteran. She wants to take it home and hang it in the theater lobby.

I call Dad. "It's boring," he says. He has said something exaggerated *and* true, and I know his thinking well enough—he often uses an eloquent shorthand—to be able to agree.

"But isn't war always boring—and exciting?" I answer.

"Oh sure," he says. "It takes you away from the inertia of your own life and seems exciting, but it really doesn't give you anything back."

Again, I *think* we have a similar take, but the point is not worth sorting out. We make plans to get together on Sunday for dinner. He tells me that the movie hasn't arrived; *Hedwig* is stuck somewhere on a truck or a train.

Courtenay just called; I can't bear to listen in. I'll get a summary from Ann.

From the beginning, Courtenay has seen how few people there have been to actually help. Today, George Bush called them "the lost." I have myself lived my life so much under the sway of illusions that I am especially resistant to anything that feels like false hope. There is a rhetoric of hope still coming out of the rescue effort, and I understand the need and reason for it. But I do not believe it. Of course I still have immense hope for my own life, and have found that believing a thing possible has proven to be essential to its getting done.

These suicide pilots are fascinating. Eleven of them trained in Florida. They moved often, sometimes once a month. They scrambled their names. When they bought airline tickets to Newark, they paid in cash and did not wait for their change. But there is also a credit card trail, and the hope is that following the money will lead back. Terrorist manuals have been discovered, with instructions about where to stab people.

After Ann gets off the phone with Courtenay, she says, "Posttraumatic stress. She's very sad and very weepy. The situation has made everybody more of themselves. Most of her friends want to leave town. She wanted to do more than she was asked to do. When she was first asked to come in, she said to herself, 'I can't do this, I'm only a third-year resident.' When she got there, the place was full of her ex-boyfriends. The ex-boyfriend bonanza, she calls it. 'Now that it's over,' she said, 'I feel that I couldn't do enough. Today I went out to buy socks for the firefighters. There was a semi from Stop and Shop and a semi from J. C. Penney parked nearby—I thought, this is silly. I bet those trucks are dropping off boxes of socks. The way everybody is dealing with the fact that everybody is dead is to feel as if we didn't do anything. One friend can't sleep; another woke up in a thunderstorm last night and called 911 to say that we were being bombed.'"

We have a dinner of sausage and vegetables, and then Ann resumes vacuuming.

◇

Philadelphia, Pennsylvania
September 15, 2001

Today we drive to Philadelphia to stay with Al Filreis.

The news reports that on Flight 93 the hijackers told the passengers that they were going to die and that they should call their families for a good-bye. People called; some of the passengers voted to fight back; the plane crashed in a field. One recorded cockpit conversation contains the repeated cry—"Get out of here!"

National Airport is still not open. Other airports are.

The Taliban is urging all foreigners to leave Afghanistan. Saddam Hussein counsels "wisdom." Fouad Ajami maintains that our adversaries are "*not* all shadowy. There *is* a return address."

Packing up from more than a month at the beach leaves me with mixed emotions. There's a melancholy in shutting down a house and in imagining it mostly empty for another year. We had perhaps too busy a time here, with so many guests, and just when we were beginning to enjoy each other the news hit. Now I am eager to get back to the world. Usually this means a return to the routines of school. This fall, because I'm on leave from Maryland, it means going back to the restaurant, dealing with the addition being built on our house, but, above all, a return to the physical presence of the people we care about. It's time to regroup.

At a press conference this morning from Camp David, Bush says, "We're gonna get 'em. My message for everybody who wears a uniform is—'Get ready.'"

Driving through New England. The low forests along the road, the clusters of pine, the sun glaring off the oak leaves. The browning grass, the scattered buttercups, the sandy shoulders. Bridges large and small, green and white highway signs, rotaries with discount outlets and lobster shacks.

The boats at anchor, at the piers on the quiet lakes. Bogs and marshes and marsh grass yellowing. The first maples are starting to turn.

Ann takes Route 88 to Westport, and we stop for lunch at The Back Eddy. The diners are mostly seniors. Ann orders fried cod; I have mine baked. The restaurant juts out into a large, boulder-strewn harbor.

I will drive now. "I feel like I'm always in a slight state of panic," Ann says, "especially when I'm driving." It's a brilliant day and the traffic approaching New York is light. I've never seen the Cross Bronx this empty. Off to the south, we can see a continuously rising cloud of white smoke. Coming into the city, the traffic had slowed, as if for an accident. But it was for a cavalcade of dump trucks parked on the shoulder. Most trucks carried flags, and the drivers were congregating at a rest stop, talking and smoking.

At around five the radio tells us that a flight attendant with her hands tied behind her has been found at the World Trade Center site.

As we drop south onto the Jersey Turnpike, New York is now on our left. Soon we can see Battery Park City, and the missing towers. We haven't exchanged more than a few words in hours.

Many flags and signs have been draped over the bridges.

Ann calls Al on the cell phone and gives him our location. It's about two hours to West Philadelphia.

When we arrive, he has made fresh bread and fresh pasta. Norma promptly gets sick on Al's front porch, and Ann disappears in order to clean it up. Al's son, Ben, is friendly and happy to serve the spaghetti and meatballs he has made. His younger sister, Hannah, is self-contained and just nods. We stay awake talking late and then crawl into bed.

Charlottesville, Virginia
September 16, 2001

Al was a student of mine at Virginia back in the late 1970s. After my final separation from Libby, Luke's mother, Al and I moved into a big brick house and lived like bachelors until I met Ann. He went on to get his job at Penn and to become a success there.

I so much admire the life Al has built. His wife left

him with two kids a few years ago, although she still lives nearby. But he is the parent of record, with a boy who's ten and a girl who's seven. His amazing energy manages to maintain a career and to keep the kids busy and happy. He has bought a house in a part of West Philadelphia that the middle class abandoned decades ago, a neighborhood now coming back. It's a beautiful three-story, with inlaid wood floors and leaded windows. Out back the neighbors share a sunny alley where they tend their gardens and live a very interconnected life. We had a salad of peppers and tomatoes from his garden.

At Penn, Al has founded a Writers House that brings in everybody from Grace Paley to John Ashbery. He has been named Carnegie Foundation's Pennsylvania Professor of the Year; his innovations in on-line teaching are spreading statewide. And he's recently finished his third book, on poetry and the cold war. Just this morning Hannah said to him, about there being so many computers in the house, some of which fell into his lap at work, "You're the most famousest and important Dad except for the president."

"We were lucky about one thing," Al says while fixing omelets. "If you're going to have a disaster, Tuesday is the best day. Then Wednesday is a dead loss; we just stare at the TV. On Thursday it's beginning to sink in. Friday we're pulling ourselves together; then there's the weekend. By Monday—maybe—we have had enough time to compose ourselves and to go back to work."

Only Al—my dear friend Al—the most cheerful man I know and the most well organized, could so soon find something "lucky" in the events of the week. And he is probably right.

While I'm talking with Al, Ann is out in the dining room on the phone with Courtenay. Courtenay has had to call Ann's cell phone; her regular line in Manhattan isn't working. "She's a mess," Ann says, when she comes back into the kitchen. "All she can do is jog, volunteer, donate money." Al says, "Yeah, she's doing the same thing we're doing—except she expected to be able to help."

"I'm not used to her being so depressed," Ann answers. Courtenay is very tough, hardened by the struggle to become a doctor and a year's worth of life in New York. "She wants to be numb, and all she can do is cry."

We say our good-byes and head south out of the city, down 95, and through Maryland, around the District, and into Virginia. A clear, warm day. In Virginia the deep green of summer is acquiring the faint cast of yellow that signals the fall. Corn still stands in the fields. The Blue Ridge looms up, on the western horizon. I'm always glad to come back to this beautiful place, where I've lived for twenty-six years.

At home we find five weeks' worth of mail and a muddy yard. In order to excavate for the addition—it's a bedroom-bathroom wing—the contractor has brought in a bobcat to run up and down our steep hill. I see a floor, stud walls, a few rafters. Windows throughout the house—most are rotten and need to be replaced—have been stripped of their trim, revealing mold and broken sheetrock. The two toilets downstairs are mildewed. Chairs and couches are covered with sheets. The porch lights aren't working; there's a Port-a-John out front. It's clear that we have come home to a mess.

Ann calls Dad, and he comes right over. He's been thinking about 1941, when he was seventeen.

"The difference then was in how slowly the news got around. I heard it early on Sunday morning, on the radio. I was supposed to take Lida to the movies, so, when I got to her house that evening, I said something about the attack. 'Oh, you're making that up,' she said. No one in the house had heard anything, and no one believed me. So we got in the car, and in five minutes we were stopped by a police road block. They let us through, and we went to Long Beach and saw our movie. *Swamp Water*. One of the worst movies ever made."

We have a dinner of corn on the cob, rotisserie chicken, mashed potatoes, and beer. Dad has baked a peach-almond cobbler. The news at the restaurant is not good; one waitress is leaving to work for the cook who just quit to open his own place; the dish washer has broken a year's worth of plates; our new grill chef has been offered a job by a man who used to cook for us. Tomorrow we have to get up and make hors d'oeuvres for a wine tasting.

"Yeah, it's probably the safest place on the planet

right now," Luke says about D.C., when I call him around eight. "F-16s still in the sky. Being in this building is funny, though. It's usually so quiet, but now everybody is home playing their TVs really loud."

"It's kind of a spidery situation. There are all these possible groups involved—but who knows? I mean I'm glad when someone like Dick Armey says things like 'Islam is a great religion and the people who did this bear as much relation to Islam as Torquemada does to Christianity.' You heard that someone killed an Arab-American today."

"I'm curious about tomorrow," Luke says, "when the markets reopen. It turns out that September is traditionally the worst time for the stock market. So is that good? Will we just have a kind of purging that we would have had a little of anyway and then start clean?"

I tell him about my fantasy that some J. P. Morgan figure calls up his broker tomorrow and just says, "Buy."

"I know the feeling," Luke says, "but something centralized like that probably won't work. We could be in for a pretty big slide."

Luke's experiences have forged an articulateness that often astonishes me and that could be mistaken for the product of a long and difficult formal education. But the fact is he left college after his freshman year. What he knows he has acquired mostly out of school, by reading. The one thing he has always accepted from me is books. This summer I lugged a fat *Norton Anthology of Theory and Criticism* to the beach. Luke began dipping into it and then showing up at breakfast wanting to discuss Freud's "The Uncanny." Maybe it's because he didn't grow up in my house that he can open himself so willingly to the world of words in which I have so happily lived.

More important: Every good conversation with Luke is another piece of evidence that he will survive.

I turn on the TV—we get only NBC—and for the first time it's not news but a regular program. *Law and Order*.

I haven't had a chance to read a paper in two days, so before bed tonight I catch up. Items of note: the chairman of Continental Airlines says, "We are all going to be bankrupt before the end of the year." Jerry Falwell has said on TV that "the pagans, and the abortionists, and the gays and the lesbians who are actually trying to make that an alternative lifestyle . . . I point the finger in their face and say, 'You helped this happen.'"

It is the fundamentalists at home that we must take particular care of.

The local news tonight in Charlottesville reports that the president has authorized the air force to shoot down any commercial airliners aimed at Washington landmarks. Cool air moving in, with towns nearby recording lows in the thirties.

Just before midnight, Ann and I climb into bed to spend the first night in our house together in five weeks.

◇

Charlottesville, Virginia
September 17, 2001

At seven we hear boots outside. Soon saws and hammers. The crew is here, and today is rafter day.

We talk a while about the restaurant and what seems like the bad behavior of the troops. Ann uses the word "betrayal."

During breakfast, Ruth comes over with our cat. Boris has been living with Ruth and Milton, our octogenarian friends, while we've been away. "We feel so blessed," she says, about not having a television. "No images." She quotes someone who has described the coverage as "compelling and repelling."

Hedwig still hasn't arrived, and Ann is dubious about its being appropriate. I mention that movie receipts for this weekend are down 44 percent from last year.

This is the day the stock market reopens. I'm away from TV all day but hear reports of a six-hundred-point drop, a rally, a drop.

After picking up supplies, we drive to the restaurant. I have never seen the refrigerator so empty: no butter, no milk, no vegetables. Then we discover that we're out of olive oil. Weeks ago we agreed to host a wine tasting on this day, so we start getting ready by making zucchini frittatas and fried cauliflower.

Then I decide to do the toast appetizer we served at

our wedding. I soften butter and mix it with sweet gorgonzola, chopped parsley, and a handful of pine nuts. I spread the mixture on triangles of white bread from which I've removed the crust. Later we will toast the pieces in batches and serve them hot from the oven.

"Whenever I eat these toasts," Ann says, "I think about getting married. Remember Courtenay serving them in her black dress and her bare feet? Cooking all that food for ninety people was the first time we acknowledged that we were about food, that we believe in our amateurness so much that we are actually going to do this for you. We accepted that how we cook was OK. And now we do it four nights a week—we produce *not* restaurant food. Except we don't ask our friends to work the grill, like we did that day."

The tasting begins slowly, but by 3:30 there are fifteen people milling about. I move next door, to the office in the theater, to type the fall menu. Who has any idea whether people will continue to eat out? We do have a group of regulars—about two hundred people—who seem to think of L'avventura as a second home, and most are middle aged, with comfortable incomes.

Ann has hung the flag given to her mother at her father's funeral in the theater lobby.

I call John Auchard, my colleague at Maryland. If you drive south past his apartment on Sixteenth Street and keep going, you'll hit the White House.

"This has been a rough time here in town," he says. "The report came in today that they will never again open National Airport. The *Post* is saying that a one-prop plane with a one-and-a-half-pound package could destroy Washington."

I ask him about the university.

"Oh, yes, it stayed open, on Tuesday. I taught all day, then wrote President Mote what I think was an eloquent letter. Of protest. Of course he canceled class the *next* day. The place is filled with gossip. And I hate the whole fucking academic idea that it's good to 'talk about things.' It's obscene if you don't know what you're talking about."

John asks about whether Luke has landed the job at an art gallery that he has been trying to arrange.

"Well, it's not over yet," John answers, when I tell him it hasn't worked out. "And I put in a good word at the Studio Theater—I believe I represented Luke as a master carpenter and the designer of the patio you built at the restaurant this summer."

"My James class is going well," he adds. " I've got a really smart black woman who began talking about 'heimlich' and 'unheimlich' the other day in class and I asked her whether or not somebody was choking. Everybody chuckled—just a little. I mean, most of us didn't know that bit of Freud from a fist in the chest. But she'll be fine—a good spirit. I've got a guy from Mexico who looks like Dick Van Dyke, a guy from China, a woman from India. I asked, rather gingerly, if she was from the 'subcontinent,' and she said 'Yes.' I kept asking until we'd narrowed it down, in her words, to 'a city named Madras.' 'Do you know it?' she asked. I looked down at my eyeglass case, which I bought in Madras, and then slid it across the table. 'Oh my,' she said, 'my father has the same optician.'"

John has done travel articles for the *Post* on India, Cambodia, and Mali. This semester he's also teaching a course on the literature of travel.

"Both of my courses are going well. They're about the globe or about America as seen by others. Just a week ago I sent my students out to do travel pieces about *airports* and also assigned a piece by Jonathan Raban about New York as a vertical culture."

John has friends on Capitol Hill who have two small sons.

"I've been on the Internet trying to get smallpox vaccines for the boys. It's a *horrible* disease. The father says that he wants to buy a gun—to shoot his kids with, in case they get it. Of course," he says with a laugh, "I've already got eighteen of the twenty-three symptoms."

I've read the *Post*'s anthrax articles and say something about there being limits to indecency.

"When you're doing anything for God," John replies, "nothing becomes indecent. I've been thinking a lot about Islam. There are certain faiths—Hinduism, maybe even Christianity—that do well under stress. Islam doesn't—it lashes out."

I mention my revenge fantasies.

"I don't have any of those. That's not in me. But

yesterday in church, this young priest got up and began ranting against retribution. It made me very angry. This has nothing to do with that—we're trying to save our world."

John is the man on whom nothing is lost. Although he takes pride and pleasure in the life of the mind, he is absolutely free of intellectual snobbery. What he detests is pretense of any kind, or what we have agreed together to call decadence—affectation, the absence of passion. I can hear already, in the tones and cadences of his voice, how immediate have been the connections he has made between the events taking place in the world at large and the little world of the classroom. And the acknowledged anger is characteristic; with my wife, John shares not just the everyday capacity to get angry but the willingness to admit to it.

At six o'clock there are twenty opened, half-drunk bottles of wine sitting in the restaurant. We finish off some Franciacorta and give some of the open bottles to our staff. One of the wine salesmen tells a story about having been mistaken for an Arab, last week, by three Virginia rednecks who muttered something about his "camel." Once he spoke to them, they saw by his accent that he was "American."

The garden at the restaurant has exploded. Orange cannas taller than I am. Marigolds the size of a small pig. My vines have grown up the new patio's cedar poles and are furiously knotting together fifteen feet in the air. Ann has harvested volunteer squash on the hill.

It's the last gasp before frost; September—here—is the ripest month.

The pilot John Ogonowski is back in the news. It turns out that in his spare time he was helping Cambodian refugees adjust to life in rural Massachusetts. When an NPR crew arrived to interview him—they were doing a story on his work before the crash—he took them out to a bluebird hatch. If you could understand this man, tell his story, and put it across to our enemies—well, we might have a chance.

At dinner Ann says, "Today I walked to places I've never been before. I took the dog to Lee Park. Then I walked down to the park by City Hall and just sat there. These are places I've never visited—but it's all I can do."

Near the end of the wine tasting, she slammed her little finger in the door to the women's bathroom. At first she seemed all right and soaked it in ice. Then she went outside. I found her sobbing in the garden. We skipped yoga and went home.

I can hear the UVA marching band practicing; we don't live far from the stadium. I don't think they've ever before played "God Bless America."

When we talk about her smashed finger after dinner, Ann admits that she was crying more out of frustration than pain. "The crying was a way of crying about a lot of things."

Courtenay calls. She's looking for her mother, who has fallen asleep. So we talk.

"Today, everybody just feels good going back to work. People come in, and whatever's bugging them just comes right out. It's all *amplified*. Now we all want to go back to our world and make the world better than it was before."

She says that on Tuesday she refused to look at "the buildings." "I had to get through it. Then I was watching *The Thomas Crown Affair*, and there they were, in the movie, and I felt heartbroken."

I ask her how it feels to be thinking about Pittsburgh, where she is slated to move next fall as a fellow in critical care.

"If I were going to leave New York, this is a good time. You know, they're going to rebuild the towers. Really. Maybe it'll be one big tower—but they're going to rebuild."

I mention that her mother found her a little shaky on Sunday. "Yup. Tuesday no tears. Wednesday no tears. No tears Friday. Saturday was the onslaught— just weeping. Sunday was better. You start to realize that everybody around you has been traumatized. And so you can't take anything they do personally; all those annoying attributes that would normally upset you don't. You know me—I went from indignation, to morality, to rage. It's true!"

"Yes," I answer, "as you say, it has made us all more ourselves. I just feel flat and withdrawn."

"Yeah, and I'm angry all the time."

We talk about her friends, about the flirty one and the quiet one. It's the quiet ones who come through.

"I told someone that she has all of my competence and none of my attitude."

"You mean she's better than you?" I ask her.

"Yes, she is."

The stock market lost 684 points today. Citizens of sixty-two countries are among the missing.

The number of missing in New York is listed at 5,422.

The number of dead in New York is 201.

The number of dead in Washington is 221.

The number of dead in Pennsylvania is 45.

A shoeless George Bush visited a Washington mosque today.

◇

Charlottesville, Virginia
September 18, 2001

The workmen are here again early this morning. They're building a hipped roof, with three angles, so it's tricky work. Loud voices at seven.

Today is Rosh Hashanah.

"Wanted dead or alive" is not quite the language I wish for from a president. I'm still struggling to accept him.

"All the synagogues are sold out." It's the first thing I hear when I pick up the phone. It's Howard Norman. He's my office mate at Maryland, a dear friend, hard at work on his fifth novel. His daughter is thirteen, and he has urban worries about her. When I mention our daughter in New York, he says, "Yes, but at least there's a sense of vicariousness for people who can in some way touch the tragedy."

Last night he found Emma at one in the morning watching CNN, tears streaming down her face.

"Your mind goes to bad places—mine went to that Japanese guy in the subway. I mean that was not part of some grand conspiracy. The BBC had an interview with an imprisoned terrorist, who said that 'all the coverage is very *instructive* to us.' Implying—we won't veer planes off route next time—we'll just hijack planes we can keep on course."

I mention John Auchard's concerns.

"Well, we're living in a targeted city. We can all make private symbolic statements, but—you know the synagogues have all hired security."

I tell him that I've been trying to keep a journal.

"For people interested in language and in thinking narratively, you have this extremely inarticulate presence—the president. Then there is, on the other side, the high rhetoric of religion. But who is speaking for us, in the middle—for quotidian life?"

Then he pauses, reminds me of how well I know him, and says, "Let me ask you a question. Would you just pack up and go to Vermont?"

I manage to say something without answering the question. I know how little Howard likes life in

Washington during the best of times, how hard it is for him to have only ten weeks a year, during the summer, in his house near Montpelier. And I'm not prepared to answer because I don't know what to think about Luke. It has been such a measure of success, to see him leave his mother's house, this summer, and to have him make a move toward independence—even if he is living in my apartment in D.C.—that the idea of needing or wanting to move him again feels inconceivable.

"People want to feel things deeply," Howard says, "so you personalize the tragedy. Who wants to be on the opposite end of that spectrum? It's not six degrees of separation—it may be one. All of these kids in our house yesterday had recently been to New York."

"With people, their hearts have moved up into their heads, as the Eskimos say."

We agree to get together on Friday, when I'll be coming up to school. During the semesters when I'm teaching, Howard and I schedule a weekly dinner where we talk about our marriages, our children, what to read. He is always passing along something. The high-water mark was in 1989, when he served as a member of the selection committee for the National Book Award in fiction. Hundreds of hardback novels began arriving at his door, many of which he handed to me. The list narrowed to five books: *Geek Love, Billy Bathgate, The Joy Luck Club, Spartina,* and *The Mambo Kings Sing Songs of Love.* We both loved John Casey's novel, and, when the prize was announced, *Spartina* had won.

Ann will be home soon. She was out early to do her radio show on the university station. I wonder what she played; it's usually Latin jazz.

The phone rings. My most intense contacts are now on the phone. It's my sister Meleesa. She is forty-three, lives with her husband and her daughter in Seattle. My favorite sister. I know she's talked to Dad a few times, but it's the first time we've spoken since September 11.

She's been experiencing a lot of strong physical symptoms. "Last Wednesday it was back spasms." Her marriage has been a struggle, lately. "I keep forgetting," she says, "that Larry's mother died this year—I know it happened. And of course it's having an emotional impact even Larry is not aware of. I'm not filled with despair to the extent that I have been. Over all, we're inching forward."

She talks a little about being estranged from Dad. She specifies the length of the breach; they hadn't talked in eighteen years until a phone call this summer. "You know, when I heard his voice on the phone, I felt regret. For the first time. About the decision I'd made, to break off contact."

She was on the phone with him last week when the second plane hit. "We had a great talk. He even made me laugh. He's always been impish, and it's as if everything has fallen away and that's left."

I say something about feeling isolated in my emotions, despite being in touch with so many people.

"Me, too. I haven't called a single friend. You're the second person I've talked to."

We talk about our youngest sister, ill in Hawaii. The third sister, the oldest, neither of us has seen in twenty years. Once Mom was killed, in the car accident, in 1971, the family began a slow scattering.

Meleesa was born when I was nine. I remember the day my parents announced the pregnancy to my sister Megan and me. It was the day before Thanksgiving, 1956. Then we went out to dinner, a rare celebration for us.

By the time Meleesa was born, the next July, we had moved to San Bernardino, to a stucco house up against the foothills. Meleesa had a thick head of black hair and huge brown eyes. Meleesa Silence Wyatt. It turned out to be an odd middle name, since Meleesa proved to be one of the most cheerful—and voluble—people I have ever known.

From the beginning, my mother included me in on baby care. I even helped to change diapers and clean them in our old ringer washer. When I fed the rinsed diapers through the rollers, my fingers sometimes got stuck, and I had to count on Megan to hit the emergency release.

I think Meleesa was the first person I loved, besides my parents, in any way that taught me about the feeling.

I went off to Yale when she was in the fourth grade. She became a great reader, the one I would send books to, and she quickly developed the desire to become an actress. Part of this may have originated from my Christmas visits home, when I organized evenings where the family read, aloud, *The Tempest* and *Saint Joan*.

Meleesa was fourteen when Mom was killed in the automobile accident. Dad moved to Laguna Beach a few years later, and she finished high school there. She acted at South Coast Rep and then at the University of Washington, where she met a dark and handsome man who took her off to New York. Her big break came when she was cast in *An Officer and a Gentleman*. She plays one of the prostitutes in bed with Richard Gere in the opening scene; the camera glides across her hip. The scene took twelve hours to film; she found him, she said, "every inch a gentleman."

A few years into the New York sojourn, Meleesa stumbled across the broken past. She wrote Dad some accusatory letters; he didn't reply. They stopped speaking, and, in 1987, when she and Larry were married, I was the one who gave her away.

At about one, Ann and I arrive at the restaurant. Our goal is to get the place ready to open after being closed for two weeks. We also plan to make a Bolognese sauce and gelato so as to get a head start on Wednesday, when we open.

A huge produce order comes in; we spend an hour putting it away. There are bills to sort through, a new menu to be typed, meat and fish to be ordered, restocking. But we get drawn into cleaning the metal shelves that run above the work space. Somehow, today, it's time to get rid of four years of grease and dirt. At five we get around to the cooking. Meanwhile, we forget to order meat. We don't get home until after dark.

The *New Yorker* came today. Ann holds up the cover, and I say, "The cover is black."

"No, look closer."

She brings it across the room. Two tall, paired rectangles, a deeper black, hidden there.

◇

Charlottesville, Virginia
September 19, 2001

The Taliban has refused to surrender bin Laden. A Soviet general who fought in Afghanistan remembers the war there as "lice, dirt, blood."

The Dow Jones lost only seventeen points yesterday. The average now stands at 8903.40. Interest rates have fallen to 3 percent.

Ann is reading an article about all the fruits that don't ripen once they are picked. Apples and peaches do; grapes and strawberries don't. "Remember those grapes we found last week, so close to the ocean?"

"Yeah, that was the best smell in a long time."

We try to work out a menu for tonight:

Starters

Grilled Shrimp with Mint–Chick Pea Aioli
Baby Greens with Citrus Dressing

Fried Cauliflower

Romaine, Gorgonzola, Toasted Walnuts, and
    Grilled Pear

Prosciutto and Black Mission Figs

Main Dishes

Baked Rigatoni

Bucatini all'Amatriciana

Roast Cod Livornese

Grilled Whole Rainbow Trout

Roast Chicken with Fall Vegetables

Today Ann is having a cervical polyp removed. I ask if I can go with her. "No, it's nothing." Then, a little later, she says: "I keep having these dreams about having to choose between having a sex life and having a life. What if they just want to rip it all out?"

"I guess we'd adjust. People seem to adjust to anything."

"I don't know—I wouldn't say that what we've been having lately feels like having a life."

"No—no," I respond. "It doesn't."

Middle age has come as a shock to us. It hit in Ann's early fifties. It hit me, too. There are no good stories about this; we feel alone with it. My close male friends who are in marriages report feeling similar things. We're surprised, and chagrined, that a corner seems to have been turned so soon. The loss of energy, of sexual desire or the ability to perform, the growing awareness that This Is It—that we are, now, surely, what we will be.

72

We have fought the ongoing physical humiliation and have had unforgettably happy moments, nevertheless.

The prevailing mood of my early and Ann's mid-fifties has been one of the sense of an ending, surely, but, more than that, of a gathering urgency. Since what lies behind us amounts to more, in sheer lived time, than what lies ahead, we have come together on the point that it is important to live our way into the future hard, before we pass into the suspect cheerfulness of old age. The unexpected result of feeling this is not a speeding up. If anything, Ann and I are content to do less grasping after experience and to let come what comes. Fewer of the moments between us feel rehearsed, or forced. And now, just as we had begun to glimpse something like wisdom, glimmering over the horizon, the world smacks the hell out of us. I am strangely grateful, even so, if only for the felt return, in recent days, of the possibility of strong emotion.

I will try to get to the restaurant by eleven this morning. If I'm lucky, I'll be home by eleven tonight.

I was wrong; I'm home by 9:30. We get slammed at 7:00, and we're done by 8:30. I dropped a dish of rigatoni, and Howard, the grill cook, burned a pizza. Forty-four dinners for our first night back.

Ann's surgery went well today—in and out. They won't know anything—meaning cancer—for a while. She and I eat the roast chicken that nobody ordered, and I call Bob Schultz in Iowa. He will be fifty tomorrow. Ann is on the phone first.

"Yeah, I did a lot of alcohol one day," I hear her say.

They talk about how they feel. Crying. Numb. Depressed. These are some of the words used.

"I even canceled a massage because I was afraid that rubbing would make me cry. I don't like to cry with other people around."

"Except me," I interject.

"Honey, I don't think of you as other people."

They agree that they can't listen to music.

Ann describes the construction project at home as a big brown hole in the ground.

Bob's department had a birthday party for him today. Near the end, someone mentioned his fear of "ethnic creep"—too many courses in African American literature, and so on. Afterward, a young black man on the faculty confided in a friend that he had never been so upset. So now Bob has to adjudicate. "There's a fiery inside," he says about the young man, "that he tries not to show people."

He's reading a book about Postville, the nearby town where Hasidic Jews have settled in significant numbers, with the predictable elbowing of the locals. They run slaughterhouses.

I mention the *New Yorker* issue and how little I enjoyed its fine writing. It is not much of a time for metaphor; "war," of course, is a metaphor. The Susan Sontag piece sticks with me; she's angry—at America—not at the terrorists. Standard radical politics, which also seem out of place, sentimental in another direction.

Henry James said about the Great War that it "has

used up words. . . . We are now confronted with a depreciation of all our terms."

And yet, more than a year later, reading another Sontag piece in the *New Yorker,* I will be filled with admiration for her refusal to reduce this war or any other to a problem of representation. "It is common to say that war, like everything else that seems to be real, is *médiatique.* . . . To speak of reality becoming a spectacle is a breathtaking provincialism. . . . It assumes that everyone is a spectator. It suggests, perversely, unseriously, that there is no real suffering in the world. But it is absurd to identify 'the world' with those zones in the rich countries where people have the dubious privilege of being spectators, or of declining to be spectators, of other people's pain."

Bob continues: "I realize that one of the bad things about war is what it does to our field of attention. We get to pay attention to so many fewer things."

We talk a little about concessions to middle age. I had worried that a phone call at nine in the evening might be interrupting something, but no such luck.

"I think we all feel as if we're running in sand these days," Bob says. I mention my side ache.

"Rounding up the usual symptoms," he answers. "I recognize my school stomach."

It's after eleven when I hang up the phone. We go to bed without turning on the news.

❖

We wake at around seven to rain. The workmen arrive, then leave. We talk about hiring a new waiter.

At breakfast, Ann tells me that "Barbara said Chris got up at four in the morning yesterday to drive to Hanscom—they're using that airport instead of Logan—to catch a seven A.M. flight. When he got there, there was something wrong with somebody's luggage, so he came home."

Courtenay says that people in New York are going to restaurants, staying five hours, and not eating their food.

Michael Kelly writes today, in an editorial entitled "We Know Who We Are," that there are "those on the left and right who hate this country for being what it is—a liberal democracy." He maintains that "we are good people and we have built what is in fact 'a just and fair and decent place,' and we will preserve this place from those who would destroy it." He puts well what I have been feeling in recent years, the continual tacking this way and that, the lack of big answers in my thinking, the support, for instance, of affirmative action in my mind along with an awareness of the harm it can do. My politics are deeply compromised. Or maybe, as Kelly might say, compromising. As a liberal democracy requires.

I find myself weeping over a newspaper editorial.

Ann comes over, stands by my chair, puts her arms around me, and is soon crying, too.

My deepest emotions—the ones that have made me cry—have not been feelings of grief. There has been some of that, of course. But when tears have been pushed out, it's been by a feeling almost akin to pride, a big swelling in the chest—of recognition—that I have an almost searing love for this country. Not, especially, for its government and larger institutions—they are fine—but of its people and its beautiful landscapes. It's a love of a particular turn in a road, where an entire mountain range swims into view, of my dear friend Bob, in Iowa, living out a decent, responsive life in such an out-of-the-way place, of the honest construction workers in my yard, who show up at seven every day to drive another nail.

Today I have business to conduct at school; it will be my first trip back since May. I drive up Route 29, east on 66, around the Beltway, and then miss the turn for College Park. I miss the second turn. When I get to work, it's a day of seeing students and cobbling together a promotion report. At six I arrive at the apartment. Luke has cleaned it up, and after I shower, John Auchard arrives. Over the years, I've introduced Luke to most of my male friends, and John is the one he seems to find most congenial, perhaps because of their easy way with self-deprecation. I make Amatriciana sauce, we drink some red wine. John is in rare form, prodigal with one-liners. Tonight he and Luke spark off each other; they are both full of cultural lore. In the apartment entryway Luke proudly displays the signed photograph of Jerry Seinfeld that John bought on eBay and gave to him.

"What's the name of that antibiotic?" John asks. Courtenay has told us that once the planes hit, the doctors in the ER began taking the strongest antibiotic they could find in case of a biological warfare attack. She told Ann that she thought against something like anthrax it would work better than a vaccine. "Tequin."

After John leaves, Luke cleans up the kitchen, and then we talk for a while. I ask him how he's feeling. "Not a whole lot. I don't have TV, so I don't have the images. Maybe—relief. My generation's bored out of its skull. There's no grinder that we've been through."

He's suspicious of the whole thing as something of a show, of the twenty-four-hour news channels and their need for event to process. But he's also aware that people are relieved to be in a situation where feelings can flow without irony. I remember something he said to Bruce Springsteen, when we got to meet him a few years ago. "Most bands come wrapped in irony," Luke said to him, "but you guys aren't like that." "No," Springsteen replied, "we're a *warm* band. Everybody has kept his health, and I've never heard them play so tight."

Luke says something else, about the people who have been propelled to the center of this thing. "People who are chemically imbalanced see their actions get stretched out and called history."

At ten he goes out to meet someone he plans to play guitar with this weekend. A sudden rain comes up; I hope he hasn't got far to walk.

◇

The first day of fall. Eighty degrees is predicted for a high today in Washington.

Luke and I share a breakfast of Pop Tarts. "Listen to that," he says, gesturing toward the radio. "NPR usually plays spiffy music between the pieces. Now it's stupid—they're trying to be so gloomy."

The Taliban refuses to turn over bin Laden. "That border is crazy," Luke says. "There are a few mapped passes and about two hundred others that only the locals know about."

Luke is down to pocket change. We walk over to Safeway and buy $125 worth of groceries. His job at the café doesn't kick in until next week.

I drive up Connecticut Avenue to Howard and Jane's house. Jane is just back from a walk; we talk about Francine Prose's *Blue Angel* and wonder why so many novels lately have dealt with sexual harassment in the academy. Howard and I then go out for lunch.

We begin with our marriages. Jane's last book of poems was called *Happy Family;* his last novel dealt with open adultery. None of this is "about" anyone's life. But we are all aware of how much of our deeply cherished domestic lives have become a source of astonishment.

The Inuit—Howard has spent some time in Canada near the Arctic Circle—have a phrase for marriage: "Stop-Go."

One reason Howard can talk with me so freely about his life with Jane is that he knows how fond I am of her. Last year, when my apartment was rented out and I had no permanent place to sleep on my teaching days, I often crashed in the double bed in Jane's study. In the mornings, Howard and Emma were out early, and over our coffee Jane and I would gossip about poets and poetry. I can still see her on our wedding day, reading Frost's "Two Look at Two" in a clear, ringing voice.

Howard recalls a scene at breakfast. Emma had made the point, about finding a boyfriend at school, that none of the candidates were "plausible." "I so much adore her," Howard said to Jane. Jane then said, "And do you adore me?"

We both agree that we need to be *told,* especially now. Howard puts it this way: "Who wants to live inside a sense of speculation?"

We talk about our reading, and lament that we can't read. Although Howard has managed to get through Conrad's *A Personal Record.*

On the drive back to Charlottesville, the radio is full of wonderful things. I listen to a speech by Ashcroft that is just plain stunning. He sounds grave, gravelly.

He calls New York "a capital of the world for spirit." To feel warmth toward a man for whose politics I have contempt reminds me of how disorderly my emotions have become.

Experts are talking about Islam. My problem is not with Islam; it is with fundamentalism. There comes a moment in every semester when I put that word on the board, and, against it, I write the word "postmodern-ism." I don't much like "postmodernism" as a word, but in this opposition it does important work. The struggle, I tell my students, is between those who believe in The One True Story and those who believe in human stories, in the huge variety of what we have all made.

I listen to a report on the cost of the terrorist operation, which may have totaled only two hundred thousand dollars. It also turns out that it won't be easy to follow the money. There is a worldwide banking operation called *hawala,* or "trust." A broker in one country holds a reserve of currency. On behalf of a client, he sends a chit to another country. The money is then disbursed. There is no check, no monthly statement—no paper trail at all. The brokers deal with each other on a regular basis—they operate on *trust*—and so they just continually net off the balance.

I arrive at L'avventura at 4:30. I type up the day's menu, take Norma home, shower, and am back by six. We are breaking in a new waiter. Early on, Courtenay calls. She has good news: she has passed her medical boards, and her grandmother, who is near the end, just sent her a check for five thousand dollars. Around eight, I have a glass of wine with Dad on the patio.

"What's happening in this country is the way gays feel most of the time," he says. He came out in his late forties, after my mother died.

"Under fire?" I answer.

"Yes. Something like that."

We talk about the burden of having feelings. He has said that the gay life, as he knew it, was routinely intense. "I would rather feel the highs even if then I have to experience the lows."

"Killing feelings is the business many people are in," I respond. "I've done it myself for many years."

I'm at home around 10:30 when the phone rings. "Cobbler?" "Sure." Ann brings home the remains, and we have a snack before bed.

◇

Charlottesville, Virginia
September 22, 2001

At the checkout counter yesterday, Luke opened an issue of *Newsweek* to a photograph of a man sitting with an open briefcase in lower Manhattan. He is covered with ash. We look harder; it is a bronze statue.

What has happened to the distinction between the quick and the dead?

On the radio, the poet Robert Hass speaks about a recurring dream in which he is digging through ashes.

Ashes. New York has become a valley of ashes, and Fitz-gerald has become a prophet:

> About half way between West Egg and New York the
> motor-road joins the railroad and runs beside it for a
> quarter of a mile so as to shrink away from a certain
> desolate area of land. This is a valley of ashes—a fan-
> tastic farm where ashes grow like wheat into ridges
> and hills and grotesque gardens, where ashes take the
> form of houses and chimneys and rising smoke and
> finally, with a transcendent effort, of men who move
> dimly and already crumbling through the powdery
> air. Occasionally a line of gray cars crawls along an
> invisible track, gives out a ghastly creak and comes to
> rest, and immediately the ash-gray men swarm up
> with leaden spades and stir up an impenetrable cloud
> which screens their obscure operations from sight.

Ann wakes up at seven this morning. She slings her leg over me and says, "Can I have some of that?" I plead early-morning sleepiness, but I'm happy to be asked. "Sometimes I just want that warm thing inside."

I will stay home today and clean our seriously dirty house while she preps for Saturday night.

At five I drive across town. The radio tells me that box cutters have been found on two more air-planes. Arrests have taken place in France, Belgium— and Paraguay.

What a strange business the restaurant business is. My dish washer just hobbled past. He's a Vietnam vet, in his late fifties. We hired George in early August and let him go because our new cook thought he had funny ideas—"paranoid fantasies." A week later we let the new cook go; he couldn't cook. The replacement dishwasher promptly stole two hundred dollars. The day we fired him, Dad hopped in his car and went looking for George. He found him down by the Salvation Army. George keeps his station clean and causes no trouble.

Tonight we did forty dinners.

Ann is downstairs running a bath.

◇

Charlottesville, Virginia
September 23, 2001

A pretty big fight last night with Ann. She's in the bathtub; I'm sitting on the toilet. She's angry with the hostess, who said to her, near the end of the evening, "We need to hire a professional chef." "A professional?" Ann answers. "Yes." "Why?" "To keep up the food quality." "Better than my food?" "Well, you don't want to keep cooking at night." It went like that. The woman is tone-deaf, and always has been.

I wasn't able to sympathize. I didn't want the sadness that follows anger to fill up the house. "She reminds me of what my mother used to be like," Ann said. When I tried to cheer Ann up, I only ended up lecturing. I went to watch *Saturday Night Live;* she went to bed.

This is why we have to sell the place.

This morning I apologize.

While we're having breakfast, Ann points to the carpet by the front door and says, "That's an Afghan rug. The rugs with the blue in them."

I spend the day typing up a promotion report and pulling together a folder on L'avventura, which will go to the broker tomorrow.

When Ann gets home from paying bills, we dress up and take a fennel and fish stew over to Reid's for his forty-second birthday. Once a student of mine at Virginia and a boyfriend of Ann's, Reid has worked at the theater for almost twenty years.

It's a house full of babies, two lovely little girls. Three-year-old Nora, who caught a glimpse of a plane hitting the building, has told her mother that there was "a storm in the city."

Nicole also teaches English, and although she loves Jane Smiley's *A Thousand Acres* and has taught it successfully for years, she's looking for a contemporary novel that might be more "uplifting."

"Uplifting is hard to find," I say. I think a while, and then suggest *The Human Stain*. "It has everything— political correctness, a burned-out Vietnam vet, the Lewinsky scandal, slumming sex, and a black man who's passing as Jewish. Roth is terrific on America's 'persecuting spirit,' as Hawthorne called it."

She has baked a cake with big pieces of apple and a

secret ingredient—orange juice. We ask for the recipe and will serve it at the restaurant.

Home by ten, we are soon sleeping.

◇

Charlottesville, Virginia
September 24, 2001

Michael Jordan has decided that he will come out of retirement and play for the Washington Wizards.

In the 1970s, the United States paid $34 million to build irrigation systems in Afghanistan that now support poppies. The FAA has grounded all crop dusters, after reports that Atta and his men paid a number of visits to a Florida airport and asked questions about how many gallons of chemicals the planes could carry.

Two pieces of business to look after today: I fax Betty Fern, the chair's secretary at Maryland, pieces of the promotion report to retype, and I call our broker to let him know that I'll be dropping off the portfolio on L'avventura.

I drive out to see the broker. We will ask three hundred thousand dollars for the business. Subtract from that capital gains tax and the broker's fee, and we will walk away with a little over two hundred thousand, not much more than what we owe. So we break even— and then pull in two thousand dollars a month in rent, as well as retaining ownership of the property. The broker thinks we can sell it within a year; I'm hoping it will happen by Christmas. I'm counting on the fact that Charlottesville is full of two things, money and vanity.

Ellen calls from Seattle. She's an old friend who introduced me to Ann. Now she's working for Amazon. She was in the hospital recovering from a hysterectomy when the attacks took place. On a trip to London, a few weeks earlier, people had repeatedly pointed to places where, over the years, bombs had gone off.

"My whole group travels a lot," Ellen tells us. "But this was one of the few times when people weren't on the road." Her son, at Berkeley, has been completely politicized by events and is connecting with the peace movement.

Ann says, "I'm going to save up all my operations"—she has a dislocated toe and may also be facing a hysterectomy—"until we sell the business."

"I'll be fifty on Friday," Ellen says.

"Oh my God," Ann answers, "I remember when you turned *forty*."

"Yes, it was the year I left my marriage." She's been on a long journey, from Charlottesville to Philadelphia to Texas to California and eventually to Seattle. About a year ago, she met a man to whom she plighted her troth under a cypress in Tuscany.

"I want to fix these things and live my life," Ann concludes. "I'm tired of being tired."

We spend an hour looking at bathtubs in a Kohler catalogue.

At 4:30 I drive across town to see Dad. He's at work on a spiritual portrait.

We chat a while about the restaurant, which he loves. He does the flowers, cleans the bathrooms, built a model for the patio that proved crucial to the finished thing. I don't have the heart to tell him that we have decided to sell it.

What am I worrying about? Dad has started half a dozen businesses, some of which didn't last more than a few years.

At 5:30 Ann and I drive to yoga class. This is our first time back since May. Class is held in a beautiful, high-ceilinged room with tall, double-hung windows on one end. There are many things I like about yoga: the chance to spend an hour being close to people I really don't know; the release of tension, which often takes the form of leaking eyes; the way the occasion marks the week. After thirty years of being a teacher, I find that yoga also provides a way of becoming a student again. Our instructor speaks to us in the ongoing present tense: "Lying on your back, and lifting the right leg. . . ." I like being talked to like this, the lack of imperatives, the verb forms arguing gently for the fact that we are already doing what we are being instructed to do.

As we fix dinner, Ann talks about Courtenay's new boyfriend. He's twenty-four, an investment banker, went to Yale. Ann and Coco tease me by calling it "Yah-lay."

"I have a good life, Mom," Courtenay has said. "I go out with my friends until eleven, and then go out with Dan and sit and talk until three. He's very sweet."

"He sounds innocent and not too dinged up."

"He's *not* dinged up."

This morning Ann talked with Phil Halapin—our therapist—about how hard it has been to come back to Charlottesville. "People here seem disengaged, as if it's not happening to them."

While we're eating some terrific Roma beans, we argue about whether an ice bath for just-boiled vegetables preserves or diminishes flavor. I invoke Thomas Keller; Ann invokes Marcella Hazan. "French cooking is about form," Ann says. "They would rather take the flavor out of something and then put it back another way than accept a mere green thing."

"It makes me feel like a failure," Ann says about the restaurant.

I resist the term.

"In this country," she goes on, "people aren't very forgiving. Success is based on longevity and money. I think I feel like a failure because I haven't been able to make it stand without us."

"Yes," I answer, "we both like to do it ourselves rather than to make someone else do it."

Phil said today, during Ann's session, that the response to undermining staff, when they make comments about needing someone "professional," is this: "You don't need to work here if you don't want to."

"Professional" is not a word I scorn, however. I think about the promotion report I had to pull together today: I said to myself, after having to rewrite the sections delegated to my colleagues, that I am working with amateurs.

And yet—the transforming cooks of the past fifty years have been amateurs, most of them women: Elizabeth David, Julia Child, Marcella Hazan, Edna Lewis, Maida Heatter, Diana Kennedy, Alice Waters, Joyce Chen, Madhur Jaffrey, Deborah Madison, Nancy Silverton. And they could all *articulate*. Their books are literary achievements, and all each really owns is its style, since—and it is a strange and wonderful thing—you cannot copyright a recipe.

As we finish up dinner, Ann says, "Sometimes I just want pasta with lots of sauce."

While she goes out to rent a video, I call Luke. "Can I call you back?" he says. "I'm in the middle of fixing dinner, and I'm starving."

Ann has brought home *Blow* and *Cruising*.

Luke calls back. "I need a cookbook, man. I'm tired of frying food. I'm like the friggin' guy in Steinbeck where I'm the man living alone that survives on fried food and the woman comes over and finds grease on everything."

"It sounds like you're eating celery."

"A few Cocoa Astros."

"With your chicken?"

"Postchicken."

Then he tells a story. "I got attacked in Ben's Chili Bowl Friday night. By this big black barrel-bodied woman. I go in there, I'm talking to two girls—the only white people in there—and suddenly I'm getting grabbed, my head and my hair. This huge chick, with those breasts that don't stop, is saying things like, 'You like black culture, you like what it does for you'—it was definitely unfriendly—like I was a colonialist, or something. She's pulling down my pants, saying things that sound like compliments but are also hostile. So I run out, and these two black dudes in a Porsche yell, 'Hop in man, we saw the whole thing.' Then they begin talking about the car as if they aren't familiar with it. Like they had me look in the glove compartment and didn't know its contents. I made my escape.—But this girl was big, man. A deep voice—she was out of control."

Luke recommends that we watch *Blow.* But the VCR is not working, so we watch *Crossing Jordan,* instead. The eleven o'clock news reports that the Airline Pilot's Association is requesting that pilots be allowed to carry loaded guns.

Charlottesville, Virginia
September 25, 2001

The *Post* headline this morning reads "Tornado Kills 2, Hurts 50 at U-Md. Campus." It rained hard here yesterday afternoon, filling our backyard stream, and as the cells moved north they intensified, and by the time they got to College Park they produced the worst storm in the area in seventy-five years. The tornado cut across the north side of campus, a mile or so from the building that houses the English department. When I call Betty Fern, she speaks with her usual calm. "We're OK. Part of campus is not OK. It came by about a quarter to six—everybody else was gone, but Chuck and I were still here. The windows in the new performing arts center are all blown out. All the big trees—most are over forty years old—near where I live were down. No classes today, but staff as usual."

Betty is a trouper, one of those people who holds a place together.

During the Civil War, Lincoln suspended the right of habeas corpus. Now the attorney general is asking permission to detain terrorists indefinitely without any means of judicial review. And he wants to be able to seize voice and e-mail messages with a search warrant and not a court order.

I read an article about an assistant professor who is offering to "give up the luxury of a relatively simple and comfortable life, including the prospect of tenure, in order to take on a more meaningful profession." He is applying for a job, that is, at the CIA.

Ann just returned from her radio show. She has been a DJ at WTJU for twenty years. "I played Jamaican jazz. I really needed a lift this morning, and it was perfect."

It's a cool blue fall day. When I come back from a walk to the UVA library, Marvin is nailing plywood on the rafters and singing to himself. "So," he says, "you catch me acting like a fool."

"It's not hard," I answer. He breaks into the huge laugh that wakes me every morning. By the end of their work day, Marvin and Johnny have almost finished nailing on the roof.

Ann comes home about three. We have tequila and tortillas, then go downstairs. Afterward, we talk about the restaurant. "I feel like there's nothing left," she says. "I don't even have time to put in an invisible zipper."

◇

Charlottesville, Virginia
September 26, 2001

Saudi Arabia has renounced the Taliban. The fear now is of a biological attack, perhaps with a truck. The FBI has charged twenty people with fraudulently obtaining licenses to haul hazardous materials.

Bob Kolker calls about wanting to return to teaching at Maryland; he left for a position at Georgia Tech a year ago and now hates it there. I promise to talk to our chair about his case.

Ann is looking bad. "What's the matter?"

"I just can't face working with those people. I feel as if no one gives me any support. I mean, Bob wants to change *his* job and everybody mobilizes. What about me?"

"What do you mean, no support? *I* give you support."

"Do you know what I talk about in therapy—leaving. I talk about *leaving*."

"That's what you do under stress."

"The only reason that I don't is that I don't trust my car."

I'm getting angrier by the minute. Suddenly I break out into a tirade—I can't help myself. I hear myself using the word "idiot." But it doesn't seem to matter. The main thing is a show of emotion. We've had this scene before. When we both calm down, we agree that I will cover more of the evening shifts. "It can't happen soon enough for me," Ann said first thing this morning, about selling the place.

I left once, years ago. I thought it was about a woman. But, looking back, I think more and more that it was about trying to get Ann's attention, or to wake us up. I caused a lot of damage, which took years to heal. We each began the hard work of changing. So, now, when I think about leaving, I know it's just a thought, a way of signaling, in my mind, some present misery.

A long day. At one I'm in the restaurant to make lamb sausage. A brief trip home, then I run the stove until 10:30.

During a break in the evening, I'm sitting in the garden behind the kitchen when George, the dish washer, comes out. He has washed dishes around town for years, walks with a limp.

"You know what happened to me?"

"No."

"Somebody tried to take my money."

"Where?"

"Over on East Jefferson. Three guys."

"So what did you do?"

"Attended to business. But when I flipped one over my head, I tore some shoulder ligaments." He fingers his left shoulder.

George mentions that he's married, which surprises me. He goes on to say that his wife is thirty. "She's bi-polar. And she was hit by a truck when she was young, so now she's on disability. We have good times."

"Two things I don't give up," he adds. "My money and my women. I should say, *woman*."

At home, Ann and I share prosciutto and figs before going to bed.

◇

Charlottesville, Virginia
September 27, 2001

The *Post* headline this morning reads "Military Strike Not Imminent." So they're taking their time. Caution seems to be winning out.

Jonathan Hayward came in for rigatoni last night. He helped us start L'avventura and then left to run his own place last January. When he comes in now, as he does every other month, what he orders is rigatoni.

Ann and I are pious cooks; we like to follow recipes. Through a series of coincidences, however, the rigatoni has become a thing of its own. Baked rigatoni involves three essential components: the meat sauce, the béchamel, and the grated parmigiano. Ann had always made her ragu in the traditional way, by adding ground beef to a battuto of finely chopped and slow-cooked carrot, celery, and onion. The next two steps are crucial, and she never varied from them. A: Once the meat is browned, add white wine to cover and cook it off. B: Once the wine is cooked off, add milk and nutmeg. Tomatoes and seasoning follow. Milk is the secret to a classic ragu, or so we had believed, the addition that gives a true sauce Bolognese its rich, rounded flavor.

A few months into our first menu, Ann decided she wanted a baked pasta with more edge. Fennel and pork were the answer. She added a head of chopped fennel to the battuto, along with a handful of ground fennel seed. Then she balanced out the beef with an equal amount of ground pork. She stuck with the addition of wine but eliminated the milk. And she doubled the usual amount of canned tomatoes. The result was a sauce redder and stronger and one that could stand up to the winds of the convection oven. Every time we take rigatoni off the menu, the clamor forces it back on.

The best thing he's read, Jonathan says, is the Susan Sontag essay in the *New Yorker,* where she argues that this was "an attack on the world's self-proclaimed super power, undertaken as a consequence of specific American alliances and actions." I think about a sentence from *The Assault,* by Harry Mulisch. It's a novel about the Nazi occupation of Haarlem, and it worries the question of resistance causing reprisal. A man who shoots a German officer and is seen to bring reprisal down on bystanders says that "The only truth that's useful is that everyone gets killed by whoever kills them, and nobody else."

And I think that he's right: if harm is done to me and I strike back, the harm does not make me strike. I decide whether to strike back—or not. My response is my responsibility.

I think of war and its metaphors. Appeasement. Quagmire. Blowback. World War II. Vietnam. Terrorism. How each metaphor seems to generate the next one, in reflexive sequence. Appeasement of the Germans at Munich originated, in part, in guilt over their harsh treatment at Versailles. Fear of appeasement led to overkill and hubris in Vietnam, which led to quagmire. Fear of quagmire led to working with the locals in Afghanistan. Once we pulled out, the Afghans filled the vacuum with their rage and all that fancy CIA training, and it, along with a lot of heroin, blew back at us.

Marvin says this morning that he and his crew will punch through the existing exterior wall of the house tomorrow or Friday. Tar paper going on the roof, soffits on the eaves.

Ann is up late this morning, talking about a salmon dish in a book called *Second Helpings,* as if nothing were wrong.

A video used as a recruitment tape for al Qaeda, produced this summer, refers to Jews as "dogs" and "pigs." It calls for a *higra,* or Muslim migration, to Afghanistan. The camera scans American bodies in Somalia, the bombed U.S. Navy base in Saudi Arabia, a state funeral in Arlington. These are portrayed as victories. Bin Laden tells his followers that "The love of this world is wrong" and that "to die in the right cause and go to the other world, that's praiseworthy."

Upscale restaurants in D.C. are down 50 to 70 percent. Business for us last week was normal for this time in September, about five thousand dollars in gross receipts.

There's an island in central Asia where the Russians left behind containers filled with anthrax. The soil nearby is riddled with deadly substances. Because of the shrinking of the Aral Sea, the island has now become a peninsula.

At five I return to the restaurant to interview a new waitress. I decide to work the patio while Barbara and Scott work indoors. Ann and Howard are cooking. From where I sit—on the cedar bench that creates one side of the patio—the view is stunning. The moonflower and morning glory vines I planted in June have completely covered the cedar framework. Through them I can see the ash tree at the corner of our little parking lot. To my left, the garden is filled with flowers, purple butterfly bushes, red zinnias, sunflowers, the last marigolds. The apple tree on the side of the hill is covered with fruit. A cloudy sky has blown in, with a cool wind. When I first arrived in Charlottesville, the English department brochure read that "The fall is long, mild, and magnificent." As it still is.

Dad called his sister in California yesterday. At seventy-seven, he's the baby in a family of six siblings. Carolyn said that Gen, the oldest, had died this summer at ninety-three. Carolyn's husband has recently been moved to a rest home. Their brother Bill suffers such a serious case of a shingle-like ailment that he can't wear clothes and lives in the upstairs of his house at a constant temperature of eighty degrees. Dad's family moved to Los Angeles from Oklahoma in 1926, and every one of his brothers and sisters has lived out a life in southern California.

Gen had stopped speaking to Dad because of his "lifestyle," he says. "But Carolyn told me that it had never made a difference to her. She's just been remembering all the good times we used to have."

Charlottesville, Virginia
September 28, 2001

When I open the front door to get the morning paper, there is Marvin, sprawled out in front of the threshold.

He must weigh at least 240 and even on the coldest days wears nothing more than a T-shirt. Today he has coordinated his shirt and his shorts.

"What a way to wake up," I mutter.

"Well, good morning to you, too," he says.

It turns out that Atta's luggage did not make it onto Flight 11. In it, investigators find a five-page handwritten document, in Arabic. Its authorship is unclear. A scholar of Islam describes it as written "by a person who lives in a delusional environment that involves a significant amount of memorized material." It is embedded in a broad Islamic devotional discourse. "Remember the battle of the prophet . . . against the infidels as he went on building the Islamic state." "Keep a very open mind, keep a very open heart of what you are to face. You will be entering paradise. You will be entering the happiest life, everlasting life. Keep in your mind that if you are plagued with a problem and how to get out of it. A believer is always plagued with problems." Then, more chillingly: "Check all your items—your bag, your clothes, knives, your will, your IDs, your passport, your papers. Check your safety before you leave. . . . Make sure that nobody is following you. . . . Make sure that you are clean, your clothes are clean, including your shoes." And, as well: "Continue to recite the Koran."

I've been thinking more about what I mean by an inner life. I suppose it comes down to the capacity for doubt, for what I call thinking against oneself. William Blake, one of my heroes, scorned doubt and called it "the bat that flits at eve" from "the mind that won't believe." But, for the most part, the tradition I know and respect acknowledges and even values doubt. "Lord I believe; help thou mine unbelief." This has always sounded to me like the true profession of faith. The split here has to do with the irrepressible will to question, and the questioning—the doubting—is what earns the belief.

But of course one believes in something. For Keats, it was the truth of the imagination and the holiness of the heart's affections. I can't think of a better way to put it. The belief I have comes from the poets. Poetry rushed in to fill the void when I lost my childhood faith. It was not a matter of replacing one set of portable truths with another; that's not what poetry has to offer.

Poetry embodies the possibility of the human act. A true act—rather than a gesture—makes something new, something beautiful and useful that was not there before: a child, a garden, a novel, a good meal. The essence of the point can be found in the etymology of the word. "Poem" comes from *poiein,* "to make." Why define poetry as above all a making? Because the poem exemplifies the gratuitous human impulse to add something to the world, to participate—as only the gods were once privileged to do—in building it out. This kind of making is what there is to do. And the poem works as the type of any such act because it issues from economy and care; its form is an extension of its content.

At 9:30 I drive over to see Phil Halapin, my therapist of seven years. Against the received wisdom, Ann and I both see the same man. "The bubble had to burst," he says, when I tell him about Luke's comment on the morning of September 11: "So it's started." I talk mostly about Ann's fears of what she'll do after the restaurant—the fear of retiring. "That's real," he answers. "It's the fear of not enough stress. There's a balance that needs to be struck between optimum gratification and optimum stress. The country's had too little stress—until lately—and Ann's had too much. But you've got to have some of it in your life."

I mention that I can't read. "I couldn't work for a few days," Phil says. "You have to be *present*. So I canceled all my appointments—except for the people who don't notice whether I'm present or not."

A morning spent writing more of the promotion report. I use words like "daring," "courageous," and "generous." Then I sit through two interviews with prospective wait staff in the afternoon. An article in the *New Yorker* called "Toque Envy" proclaims the end of sauté as the glamour station. The hot new station is the grill—we have a huge Montague grill at the restaurant, fired with hardwood charcoal made in Quebec. The article also maintains that the best chefs are not classically trained. Dad brought Ann the article yesterday. "He's so good," she sighs, "at supporting the wayward and the flagging."

Tonight I cook from 5:30 until 10:30—at the stove. I forget little things, like the garlic in the spaghetti and scallops and the potatoes in the Ligurian fish stew. Ann is off doing a benefit for women's health at Escafé; she has made eggplant lasagnette. A little Jay Leno when I get home, then I climb into bed.

◇

Charlottesville, Virginia
September 29, 2001

I sleep late. Around eleven, Bob Schultz calls from Iowa. Last summer during our visit he took us out to a trout stream north of town, where he plans to go again today. He lives in the "driftless area," where glaciers didn't flatten the landscape, and the bluffs and valleys in his corner of the state harbor little, meandering rivers full of brown and rainbow trout. Bob's a fly fisherman; he catches the trout and then throws them back.

He is working long days as chair but says that he finds it hard to concentrate on a task. "My mind just flits around. But I have enjoyed working with people, to ease their—situations."

It is now estimated that the terrorist operation led by Muhammed Atta cost more than five hundred thousand dollars and was run out of Hamburg. Ann says, "It's clear that's where you go when you want to foment. Didn't the Beatles get their start in Hamburg?"

I'm spending a quiet afternoon when Dad calls from the theater. "Your wife says you have forty reservations, and she wants you to come in and stand by in the kitchen. I'm sorry—I called the Red Cross—but they wouldn't help."

So tonight I expedite while Ann cooks. I assemble the beet and arugula salad, the gnocchi with tomato and mushrooms, the cheese tray, the chocolate gelato sundaes. The evening goes smoothly; we do close to seventy dinners. But I'm tired to begin with; sleeping doesn't seem to do much good lately. Sometimes I feel as if this place is eating me alive.

◇

Charlottesville, Virginia
September 30, 2001

Ann's benefit dinner on Friday night was a big success. She was in the kitchen with two other women, one who did a pork loin wrapped in prosciutto, the other who prepared grilled calamari with heirloom tomatoes. Both work in local restaurants, although neither is an owner. But they talked easily together and made her feel as if she really does have peers. Running a restaurant, for Ann, has been *lonely*. She often complains that there aren't any women around she can talk to—that the kitchen is too "male." She's as self-taught as they come in a town full of people who live and die by credentials.

I'm trying to remember this morning the six "world-views" that some historian claims are now likely to find themselves in conflict: Islamic, Slavic-Orthodox, Confucian, Hindu, Japanese, and Western. That's it. Not much on the list has to do with national borders.

"I think Muhammed Atta and Al-Shehhi were lovers," Ann says this morning. "There's a story about this woman who gets into a fight with Muhammed over a cushion and he almost decks her until Al-Shehhi comes between them." The two men shared a room in Hamburg and took flight lessons together in Florida. One was genial and one was brooding. Foot soldiers in al Qaeda were instructed to pack cologne in their luggage so that they would "look like" they were interested in women.

We talk about the power of homoeroticism in a culture so oppressive of women. "The other night, at the benefit," Ann remembers, "Rachel talked about how oppressed she had been in kitchens and how she would go home at night and cry. But when I read about places where they cut off clitorises, I think that we have it good."

A *Post* article with a flow chart of the terrorist cell, now seen as one interconnected group, with this heading: "The conspiracy was built out of the most ordinary things: apartment leases, hotel reservations, car rentals, drivers licenses and airline tickets. . . . The steady presence of Muhammed Atta, an acknowledged leader of the group, can readily be seen. The records also indicate two distinct classes of hijackers. At the top were the pilot-leaders who entered the United States earlier and took flight training; beneath them, the foot soldiers who came later and spent their time in gyms." Now it's assumed that there was only one pilot on each plane.

For Sunday breakfast—which we have at 1:30— Ann makes Irish soda bread scones. We dance around the living room to Ernest Ranglin and Monty Alexander while the scones bake. "See, your life's not so bad," Ann says. Then she goes back to watering her orchids. "Returning to your first love," I say. "No," she smiles, "Norma's my *first* love."

Today we're driving out to see Jahan Ramazani and Caroline Rody. Along with Al Filreis, Jahan is perhaps my most successful student. He took two courses from me at Virginia in the late 1970s. I gave him an A+ in the first one, the only such grade I've given in my years of teaching. One of the few freshmen in the class, he somehow assumed that he was supposed to *memorize* the poems assigned. Jahan went on to a Rhodes scholarship at Oxford, a Ph.D. at Yale, and then a return to Virginia, where his father had taught for forty years in the Department of Government. His current project is to re-edit the *Norton Anthology of Contemporary Poetry;* he's replacing Richard Ellmann. I couldn't resist passing along a list of poems and poets I'd like to see make the cut.

Jahan's family is from Iran—Persia, he also likes to

say. Caroline is Jewish. They have two beautiful, black-haired sons, one four, one eight months.

When we arrive, Jahan insists on a soak in the hot tub. He tells me that the university president asked him to read at a memorial service. He chose three poems by Auden, "September 1, 1939" and lines from the elegies to Yeats and Freud. "Auden's the one," I agree, "when you want a poetry of public grief."

We're sitting on top of a mountain with a view toward the Blue Ridge. Jahan grew up in Albemarle County and always wanted a view. Home renovations come up, and Ann says, "Dave had to apply for a summer grant this year in order to pay for our hot tub."

"Yes," Jahan responds, "and I had to do the *Norton* to buy four acres on the side of the hill."

Ann calls it "The Ramazani Purchase."

Jahan is scheduled to fly to Houston in a few weeks and is a little concerned. American born and bred, Jahan is a handsome man with the receding hairline and the bronze skin of his clan. I doubt that anybody alive cares any more than he does about English poetry. But he does have the Persian looks and the Persian name. He thinks it will be wise to carry his passport. "I called and asked for a paper ticket," he says. "But still, somehow, you find yourself feeling like a criminal."

At nine Ann and I drive over to Vinegar Hill to watch *The Princess and the Warrior*.

◈

The Taliban now admits to sheltering bin Laden. He is being kept "in a place which cannot be located by anyone."

A day spent finishing the endless promotion report. Having myself been turned down for tenure at Virginia, in 1980, I'm perhaps oversensitive to the rhetorical demands of the occasion. The tone is understated, with a sprinkling of over-the-top adjectives.

At a tile store in town, Ann and I get dizzy at the choices. The saleswoman has a guru-like star in the middle of her forehead. Fortunately we've fortified ourselves with burgers and fries at the Riverside, the only place in Charlottesville where we still eat out.

For years, in yoga, my formal focal object has been an original Peter Max oil painting of the Statue of Liberty. There are many paintings within it, fields of brushy color that look like a de Kooning or a Hoffman. A brilliant crimson around the coppery-green head, with the crown and the features in an inky black. Tonight I stare and stare at the unsmiling face as I try to keep my balance.

After yoga we repair to the restaurant, where we grind up a few legs of lamb. Dad and Ann roll little piles of meat in plastic wrap; we poach the bundles and end up with eight pounds of lamb sausage.

The recipe is simple, and of my own devising.

Grind four to five pounds of lamb—either shoulder or leg—along with a pound of pork fatback and half a pound of pancetta. Add a handful of fresh thyme, a tablespoon of black pepper, some chopped garlic, a generous teaspoon of red pepper flakes, a little salt. Sprinkle with white wine to moisten, and shape.

◊

Washington, D.C.
October 2, 2001

I hate being asked to observe colleagues teach. It's the perfect proof of the Uncertainty Principle, where the observer always interferes with the result of the experiment. But my tenure candidate needs testimony on his behalf, so by eleven I'm sitting in English 301, the gateway course for the major, watching twenty-five students discuss August Wilson's *The Piano Lesson*.

I'm off to Maryland by eight. Before I leave, Ann says, "The new thing that bothers me is that something terrible will happen and you won't be there. I'm very hesitant to do anything this fall that takes me away from here." Separation has become the issue, and I've become more aware than ever before that in this country we must often find the will to care for each other across vast distances.

The people who make the little bags of peanuts given away on airplanes make 300 million a year and have laid off half their workforce.

In the halls at Maryland, I run into John Auchard. "You ought to go to the museums on the Mall," he says. "There's nobody there."

"Is it because people are afraid—or deflated?"

"That's just it. It's a death. You're in mourning. So I'm spending more money than ever before in order to support things. I'm sick of my honors students, by the way. Can you believe it?—they find Joan Didion 'boring.' They think she's a name dropper—all those French words."

A dinner at Arugula with Howard, Jane, Emma, and friends. Jane is a poet, and a man at the table is the current poet laureate of Maryland. We all love poetry. So they all have strong opinions about Jahan's anthology. I tell them that after the attacks he has found his imagination drawn to the great moderns—Yeats, Stevens, Eliot, Auden. The only one since who measures up, he said, is Heaney.

"What about Bishop?" Jane asks, incredulously.

"I have been arguing hard for 'Crusoe in England,'" I say. "By my lights it's the biggest poem of the second half of the century. And what could be a better poem for right now—it's so much about loving the other, or discovering that the other is really the same." *Mon semblable,—mon frère.*

Two winters down the road, when Jahan's anthology appears, "Crusoe in England" makes the cut.

After dinner, I drive down Connecticut Avenue to the apartment. Luke comes in around nine. He tells a story about walking down by the White House. "Suddenly forty cop cars showed up. Then a long line of black SUVs came by—it must have been Bush. They use a lot of decoy vehicles. I was standing on the curb watching and these D.C. bicycle cops come by and pushed us back."

We talk about operating in Afghanistan.

"I read this great article in the *Times* magazine. The guy opens by saying, 'The last haircut I had was in Kabul.' The way he tells it, you're going to feel a lot of temporal vertigo there. Guys on donkeys carrying beat boxes. Boys who carry machine guns using eye liner. A real fascination with things American, and a hatred, too. The only way to do it would be to drop in a small group of Special Forces. I mean, we train those guys by dumping them in the ocean off Alaska and then making them swim twenty miles and take photographs. I bet we've got some guys operating out of there right now."

We walk down to Tamarindo, and Luke inhales a beef burrito. Adams Morgan is filling up with cheesy bars.

Before going to bed, we talk about the pennant race. Luke is a Mets fan.

"Seattle looks unstoppable," he admits. "They play as a *team*. Although with the Yankees it's going to be 'Let's win one for New York.'"

We wonder what it is—weight training, smaller stadiums, a new ball—that accounts for this year's record number of home runs.

Charlottesville, Virginia
October 3, 2001

This morning Luke says, "I can't read the paper every day, it bothers me."

"Why?"

"It makes me fucking angry." He's also worried about cross-contamination between art and journalism. "I was thinking about a situation in which you get your paper and open it feverishly and it morphs into *War and Peace,* and then later you open up some tome and it just contains trivial news." *War and Peace* is one of the books Luke read during the year he lived in Charlottesville, in his own apartment, after dropping out of high school and before going off to Bard.

When I go out to my Corolla to fetch the dishes Dad has bought for Luke, I find the right rear back window broken in. They have taken the box of dishes and my briefcase but have left a bottle of wine lying on the floor. Luke comes down to photograph the damage, and then I drive to 16th Street to pick up John Auchard, who calls the incident a "minor horror."

He wants to try coffee at Sparky's, the café where Luke is working. We sit outside and talk about the new appetizer he's discovered: fingerling potatoes stuffed with Asiago cheese, butter, mayonnaise, and themselves—mashed. He distributed the recipe to his

James class. "This is all part of their education," he says. "Ooh—*mayonnaise*," one of the students chirped.

After his recent trip to Mali, he's thinking of doing a course on Henry James and Africa. "The culture I saw there had a strong sense of the parameters of behavior," he says. "Mali definitely has a high culture aesthetic. It puts a premium on dignity—on carriage. The *Post* wants me to take another trip, by the way."

I mention Uganda, since we both know a bright student with possible connections there.

"No, I'm afraid Africa is off limits for a while. The *Post* wants me to do China, something its advertisers can get behind. I met someone from the *New York Times* last week, and he told me revenues in the Travel section are down almost 80 percent."

After dropping John at his apartment, I drive toward the Mall. I'm heading west on Constitution when an eerie replay of Luke's experience occurs. A motorcycle cop signals me over. Six more cop cars speed by, sirens going. They're followed by a caravan of black limos and SUVs. In one I see a man in Arab robes, staring straight ahead.

I park near the State Department and walk over to the Vietnam Veterans Memorial. It's a warm day, and by the time I reach the bottom of the memorial the heat is blazing off the black granite. The dates read 1959–1975. America's longest war.

It's my war, the one I did not get to fight. Instead, I tried to stop it. I have utterly no regrets about this; we did not understand either our ally or our enemy. I applied for conscientious objector status, but before the local board had time to rule in my case the first draft lottery, held in the fall of my senior year at Yale, rendered the question moot. I drew number 235 and was then free to marry and to go on to graduate school.

As I stand at the bottom of the memorial and look out, I remember again that one wing points directly at the Washington Monument and the other points directly at the Lincoln Memorial. These wars—these American stories—are interconnected, the positioning of the memorial seems to argue. I complete the circuit and walk toward the river.

At the Lincoln Memorial, the signs read "Quiet—Show Respect." It's the Second Inaugural Address, carved on the inside right wall, that I've come for. I want to see that sentence again, up in stone. It falls at the end of the second paragraph of the speech. Lincoln begins by talking about how long the war has lasted, about its unpredictable outcome, about the events that led up to it. Then he writes: "And the war came."

And the war came. For my money, it's the greatest sentence to come out of the Civil War. Four words, four syllables. The voice moves quickly over the conjunction and the article and catches on the word "war"—it's an extended syllable. Then the voice breaks on the long vowel of *came*. The sentence makes it sound as if the war were a thing that could not be stopped or helped. In the awful inevitability of the claim, Lincoln places its causes and outcomes seemingly beyond the scope of human control.

And yet—cannot the sentence also be read as arguing the opposite case, the case that the war came as the terrible earned consequence of the eighty-five years of United States history that preceded it?

Then I read on and see a sentence I had not remembered. Lincoln proceeds to talk about the nation's population of slaves. He describes this population as constituting a "peculiar and powerful interest." He then makes the following claim: "All knew that this interest was somehow the cause of the war."

I had a chef at L'avventura, Virginia born and bred, who once said to me that the Civil War was not about slavery—it was about state's rights. The claim outraged me, but I held my tongue. Combatants in all wars use the language of principle as a cover for the operation of interests. Any careful reading of the historical record will show that slavery was somehow the cause of the Civil War. There was a high correlation, for instance, between slave holding and votes for secession in the counties of Virginia. Counties with slave populations of only 2.5 percent or less voted three to one against secession, while elsewhere, in the counties where slaves amounted to more than 30 percent of the population, Virginians supported secession by ten to one. Virginians, in other words, voted in the direction in which their interests lay.

Lincoln has one more thing to teach me this day. It's

a point about prayer. As he nears his close, he considers the paradox that in this struggle between two sides, "Both read from the same Bible and pray to the same God and each invokes his aid against the other." I want no invocation of God in any fight to which I am a party. This has nothing to do with believing in God, although I don't. It has to do with facing up to what I'm fighting for. I'm fighting not for an ordained good but for my country's unique set of historical *interests*. These are valuable—supremely valuable, to me—and worth fighting for. And this kind of fight is terminable, while a holy war is not. As Lincoln goes on to say, "The prayers of both could not be answered."

Back in Charlottesville, the answer phone carries a message from a woman in Adams Morgan who has found my papers on the street. I call Luke, and he runs over to get them. "Your green sweater is here, too," he says, when he calls back.

Today Ann fired the hostess who has been with us since we opened. She has seemed profoundly unhappy and expresses it by being hypercritical. I arrived at 4:30 and typed up some menu changes. Ann had prepared a little speech and written a severance check. She met D. in the parking lot. "It was hard," Ann said afterward. "She said, 'So you're firing me because I'm depressed.' Well, I didn't exactly deny it. Then she said that she had never gotten over the wine incident."

About a year ago, wine began disappearing from our underground, and Ann posted a note on the refrigerator threatening to prosecute anyone caught taking it. We also changed the lock on the cellar door. "But I gave you the key," Ann said.

I stay out of the way until it's over. Then I have to tell Barbara, who works with D. two nights a week. "We had to let D. go today," I tell her. "It was hard; I know that the two of you were close. It's not appropriate to say any more about it. But I hope you'll stay." Barbara doesn't appear to register experience; I can't tell anything from her face. "Actually," she answers, "I may be leaving Station. I'd like more work." We agree to sleep on it.

Dad drops by and informs me that this morning Ann was voicing second thoughts. "Am I doing the right thing?"

"You've stopped loving yourself, I told her," he says. "You have to forgive yourself for getting into this position."

"You're right—I'm feeling guilty."

"You just feel guilty for giving everybody a second chance."

Charlottesville, Virginia
October 4, 2001

Struggling with a new dish yesterday, Howard Griffin, our grill cook, said to Ann that after his big car accident he is used to dealing with pain. "I've always been a masochist."

"Howard, in order for there to be an M, there has to be an S."

"Oh, you mean I can't just be a masochist?"

I'm on the computer when the HVAC man asks me to position our heating ducts. I'd like to reduce their number, but the technician says, "The boss would kill me if I did that." It's the same boss who designed the system at the restaurant, one so overbuilt that we started calling him Aeolus. God of the wind.

On the four o'clock news, a report that a chartered Russian airliner out of Tel Aviv has exploded in midair and fallen into the Black Sea—which is three thousand feet deep. The possible explanations are two—either the plane was hit by a stray missile from a Ukrainian military exercise, or it was blown up by a bomb. Israeli officials reject the second notion, saying that there was no breach of security in Tel Aviv. The Ukrainians are saying that one of their missiles could not have traveled that far.

And yesterday, a Croatian with a lapsed visa riding on a Greyhound bus in Tennessee slit the driver's throat, took the wheel, and crashed into a field, killing six. The driver survived.

The training of a second new waiter goes well tonight. He's forty and has decided to become a blacksmith. He brings blacksmith hands—the permanent dirt under the nails. "I wash and wash," he says.

"I don't mind," I reply. "Working hands."

Around seven, I spell Ann on the stove and cook the

rest of the night. Later on—it's a warm night, with today's highs in the eighties—we share a spaghetti with garlic and oil on the patio. Ann tells me that the hostess we just let go has been dating the cook who left in August to open his own place.

Charlottesville is a town small enough, and one so tightly knit, that it can recycle many of its restaurant personnel, most of whom move on every two or three years and some of whom even end up back where they started, none the richer but certainly a little older as the price of the transit.

In Houston today, Barry Bonds hit his seventieth home run. Elsewhere, Ricky Henderson eclipsed Ty Cobb's record of career runs scored.

◇

Charlottesville, Virginia
October 5, 2001

"I'm never doing another marathon show," Ann declares this morning, as she leaves the house. "I love doing my weekly show, but I hate the marathon. All that whining for money." She is scheduled to be on the radio from nine to noon today, but somehow the jazz director managed to omit her show from the printed program.

In the paper this morning, I read, with shock and chagrin, that Gregory Hemingway, Ernest and Pauline's second son, died at sixty-nine yesterday, in a jail cell in Miami. A physician, he married four times, like his father, suffered from depression, like his father, and is believed to have undergone a sex change operation. He died in the woman's section of the jail, after having been arrested in Key Biscayne for indecent exposure. *Papa,* Gregory's memoir, is not a bad book, of its kind, although it holds the father a little too responsible, it seems to me, for the life difficulties of the son.

Ann has decided to play Brazilian jazz. I call her at 10:30 to make a pledge. "How are you doing?"

"Great. I've made almost three hundred dollars. Maybe I should always be dropped from the program. Brings out the sympathy vote."

Bob Schultz calls. "I'm taking a sick day. Although I will go in for a 1:30 class. Today I'm re-reading *The Apology.*" Luther College requires a unit on the Greeks.

"Does it do any good these days?"

"Well, Socrates is so cantankerous and radical in his devotion to knowledge, with all the cross-questioning of his listeners, that students initially dislike him. And then they get into the second half of the thing and see what he stands for, and it shakes them up."

I describe my life: the restaurant, the renovation, the promotion report, and the trips to D.C.

"You must feel as if you're sitting in the eye of change," Bob says.

"Well, I spend most of my time thinking and feeling about the crisis."

"I think I'm doing the alternative. I'm occupied by

the immediate tasks of the day. Then at night I have completely literal dreams about buildings falling and fire in the streets. So I suppose you experience it either consciously or another way."

"At a distance," he goes on, "your imagination can do only so much with images on a little box. To stand and actually look up at the rubble, that would be pretty shattering. Here, one can't quite get the dimensions."

I ask him what he's reading. He's just getting around to *The New Yorker,* and, inevitably, the Sontag piece comes up. "Everything she says is true, I suppose. But it's so ill timed, so rhetorically inappropriate, so blind to the immensity of suffering among our immediate kin, that it's just—inhuman."

"Are the Greeks any more use to you?"

"Well, we always have to do the Peloponnesian Wars. And there is this astonishing dialogue in which the Athenians are dealing with the Melians, on their little island. The Athenians simply mean to take over. 'The strong rule where they may, and the weak submit where they must.' There's this striking contradiction between the openness of Athens as experienced from within and its imperial presumptions when it faces outward. I let my students draw the parallels."

"I read part of *The Republic* this summer," I respond, "and despised it. He's such a Puritan. He casts out realism because it tells it like it is; he wants art to represent ideals. As if people ever learn anything from being told how they ought to behave, as opposed to being challenged to own up to how badly they really can and do behave. He's dead wrong, and Freud knew it. He knew that illusions make us sick, and that facing up to reality—even the very worst of it—is what makes us strong."

"Well," Bob answers, "Plato was a child of the wars. He saw Athens fall apart, and it made him spin out a dark and desperate philosophy. He becomes a tyrant, an antidemocrat. He's also the original dualist; he gives us the whole mind-body split."

"It's the poison at the heart of Western civilization," I say.

"Yes, and it's what Lucy is struggling with. She hates Plato. She's trying to get around dualism. So she's been reading Hegel, of all people. She seems to think that there's something in his notion of dialectic that will take her where she wants to go. And she's taking a dance class, which moves her back into her body."

We talk about the claim that September 11 marks the true beginning of the twenty-first century. "I've never seen a culture flip over from decadence to the next page in a day," Bob says, "but it happened. The thing that keyed this for me was that benefit concert, the second week. It started with Springsteen. A dark stage, then lights up, candles, and Bruce standing in front of the band. 'My city in ruins, my city in ruins, my city in ruins. Take these hands, take these hands, take these hands. Rise up—rise up—rise up.' It went something like that. That's when the page turned; that's when we got serious again."

Ann makes $450 on her marathon show.

After a cardboard recycling trip, I run into Reid on the Mall. We talk about sleep without rest.

"It's absolutely the worst time for Nicole," he says. "Her hormones are going crazy anyway, with the breast feeding. So it's all *danger*. She's the one stomping her foot to the floor every time we drive anywhere."

We're both looking to refinance houses; Reid's may become too small, with the two girls, and when we bought Dad's, last year, we signed on at a rate of 8.75 percent.

It seems as if the last time we saw Reid and Nicole free from the busyness of the restaurant and of child-raising was back at the pasta trials in 1996. We asked them over to do a tasting of four different commercial pastas—Barilla, Molina, Delverde, and De Cecco. As I sat them down, I told them this: "Tonight, with flavors, we'll be moving from the simple to the complex. But don't focus on the sauce—focus on the noodle. You'll be tasting blind. Look for four things: Integrity, Tooth, Taste, and Loft."

De Cecco won and has been our house pasta ever since. None of the sauces we used—basic tomato, aglio e olio with watercress, leek and lemon, and cauliflower with tomato—made the eventual menu.

At the restaurant tonight, things go a little crazy. As the evening begins, I find George in the parking lot, having a fight with his wife. "Just come home tonight!" she yells at him. I'm the host, with Courtney the new waitress inside and Scott on the patio. We're empty until seven, and then we get slammed. A man on the patio beckons me over and says, "At the prices you charge, why such shitty napkins?" I explain that you get paper outside and cloth inside. It throws me off, and I never regain my balance.

Our best customers—he's the head of pediatric oncology and she teaches Spanish—wait forever for their appetizers, so I make sure their mains come up fast. They won't hear any sort of apology. "We have to try to enjoy these last few warm evenings," Pedro says.

During staff meal, Ann tells a sad story about the trout. It's beautiful trout, fresh rainbows that we grill whole over the coals. Ellen brings us about fifteen boned trout every week, for $2.95 apiece. We sell a trout for fifteen dollars, and it's so good we've never taken it off the menu. But now they're in short supply, Ellen says, because during the days following September 11 two million trout eggs died while the planes weren't flying.

◇

Charlottesville, Virginia
October 6, 2001

"Don't leave the job unfinished like you did in Iraq." This from Iran this morning, on our efforts to get bin Laden.

Atta's will has been discovered. The detailed burial instructions require the person who washes his body to

124

wear gloves "so he won't touch my genitals." He bars "a pregnant woman or a person who is unclean" from visiting his grave.

This morning in bed, Ann says she woke in the night and said to herself, "Oh my God, I've completely forgotten Dave's birthday. It just went right past me." My birthday is tomorrow.

Dad asked her if he could buy me a new pair of sweat pants. "Sure, it'll go with what I'm getting him. His request."

"What's that?"

"A broom." I did ask for a broom; the house is in a constant shambles.

My recent daydream is of a giant snow storm that will stop everything for a few days.

In the afternoon, I vacuum the house and clean the bathroom. By 6:30 I'm back at the restaurant to help expedite. Ann tells me Courtenay has called.

"She says everybody in New York is obsessed with anthrax. A new boyfriend, who works at ground zero, is very worried. But if anything had been brought in on these planes, she says, we'd all be sick or dead by now."

Near the end of the evening, I ask Howard to make a pizza for Dad and myself. We grill our pizza over the coals—you have to spread the dough with your hands, flip it on to the grill, toast it, pull out the grill, flip the pizza, dress the grilled side, push in the grill, and toast the other side. Howard makes a big, beautiful pizza with huge rounds of sliced tomato, grated fontina, and a zigzag of red pepper puree. After eating a piece, I slip into the kitchen and whisper to Ann that I think it's time to up his salary. She agrees.

"Howard," I say, "this pizza is so good we're going to give you a raise."

He grins, as if we're joking.

"No, we're serious." Then I return to the dining room, leaving Ann to spell out the details.

Somehow weight lifting comes up—Luke lifts every day—and Dad tells me a story.

"You probably don't remember the one about the guy next door, when I was growing up. He was so skinny you could barely see him. It got so bad that he became anemic, or bedridden—I forget which. Well, it came out that he had been beating his gourd ten times a day. It even weakened his heart. So—he decided to change. He took up weight lifting. He became so magnificent, it was incredible. After that, he came over and had me do it for him.—I was a kid, what did I know?—Life didn't really work out for him, though. Two failed marriages, couldn't hold a job. He had done all right in the army, during the war, so he decided to re-enlist. He was one of the first to be killed in Korea. But I remember something he said once, when somebody commented on his bad luck. 'I had as much of a chance as anybody.'"

◇

Ann wakes up this morning and says, "Sometimes I don't know what you really feel about me."

"You don't? That's sad."

"Well, I mean you make all these comments about sex, but it's not as if you really want that much of it."

"It's just a way of talking. Of voicing the sense that things are changing—that we don't have time to enjoy each other."

"You know, sometimes I'm over at Integral Yoga and I see these couples, about our age, and I'm moving with all deliberate speed, with the wind at my back, and she's saying to him, 'Do you want to try this?' They're looking at nuts, and at dried fruit, just wandering around. And I think I would hate that—just browsing for beans."

How do I feel about Ann?

Like she saved my life. When I met her, in my early thirties, I was depressed without knowing it, obsessed by the academy, demoralized about sex, and badly dressed. The only thing we haven't been able to work through is my indifference to clothes.

So I'm grateful. Beyond that, I'm engaged and attracted. Ann is incapable of saying a dull or witless thing, and, despite the widening that has come to both of us with the years, she has kept her lovely ins and outs. Just seeing her gives a boost to my passion and my morale.

I remember a day in the garden outside the theater, in the year we were building the restaurant. Early spring sunshine. Ann locks her knees and bends from the waist, over some kale that has wintered over. Pink rises in her cheeks. Her black hair, now shot with gray, shines almost purple in the watery light. She digs a little, the world stirs for me.

We have been together nineteen years. In a world without heaven to follow, I can think of nothing more sacred than going through time together.

Today is my fifty-third birthday, and Dad has invited us over for brunch. A blazingly clear fall day.

Cal Ripken played his final baseball game last night, in Baltimore. *He* had a wind at his back.

Mohammed Atef, a former Egyptian policeman, has been identified as a key planner of the attacks. We have placed a bounty of five million dollars on his head. The operation kicked off last year with a transfer of one hundred thousand dollars now traced to the United Arab Emirates. More than half the FBI team on the case is dedicated to tracking the money. In a recent interview, bin Laden said, "Al Qaeda comprises of such modern educated youths who are aware of the cracks inside the Western financial system as they are aware of the lines in their hands."

Somehow coffee this morning devolves into a fight. It's the usual fight—I'm pushing too hard and Ann feels pushed against. She's right, but it feels as if old ghosts play into it, too. I go out for a walk, and then we make it up.

Courtenay calls. A package for me is on the way from Old Navy. Her brother has come for a whirlwind visit. "I feel like New York is my own personal spa," she says. They've had a great time; she attended his gig in the Village, where his trumpet playing sounded terrific; a brunch of steak and eggs; and shopping for Ian's son Gabriel at F. A. O. Schwarz.

"I think I just saw you drop a hundred dollars in an hour," he said to her.

"Oh, that's nothing. Last weekend I spent five hundred."

Luke calls. After best wishes, he says, "I hate to rain on your birthday parade, but I lost my wallet last night." He launches into the evening's saga.

"I went to a party—this guy was serving bratwurst and other stuff. At one point he put on a George Carlin video—made before the attacks. And it was about airport security. Carlin even mentioned box cutters. So I got on his case, and he turned it off. Then we went to the Black Cat. After that, another party. A Jacuzzi scene there; a kind of orgy. The water looked sort of dirty, so I hesitated. Then I got drawn into talking with this sixteen-year-old kid whose brother had brought him to the party and then taken off—a real cool kid. By the time I got into the hot tub, it was too late for anything. When I got out, my wallet was gone. I had people looking all over with flashlights, but no luck. It's not a big deal—just six dollars and my IDs. And my weekend's list of phone numbers. I like to clear the list every Sunday. It's not like George's wallet—remember that *Seinfeld* episode where he's sitting in a booth, and he takes out his wallet and loses three inches?"

We drive over to Dad's for a little party.

"You haven't heard the news?"

"No."

"We started bombing an hour ago. Bush said we will bomb tonight and drop food tomorrow."

CNN carries the familiar fuzzy green picture; it's night in Afghanistan. We are bombing six or seven targets, including Kabul and Kandahar. Cruise missiles, bombers, fighter planes. The attack started at 11:45 Eastern time.

Dad has made scrambled eggs, toast with scallions and cream cheese, a fruit relish. For dessert, he has purchased a chocolate bombe.

Back home, we are suddenly exhausted. We fall into bed and wake up at 7:30. "I feel as if I'm being held together by nervous tension," I say. "But there is a sense of being alive that goes with it, a feeling of reawakening."

"I guess I didn't think we'd have to do this," Ann answers. "The way we did it in the Gulf War. I found that unsatisfactory. So cowardly."

I think about our history with air war, the desire to take effect at a distance.

We're dropping food, medicine, and supplies in

northern Afghanistan. The temperature there is in the low to mid-forties.

I put on the sweat pants and top Dad bought me, and Ann says I look like a teddy bear.

Meleesa calls from Seattle. "The theater is really on thin ice right now," she says. "People aren't signing up for classes. We're trying to see if we should do the show; it's a Neil Simon called *The Good Doctor*. Way more Chekhov than Simon."

Half the money in the theater's reserves will get spent to produce the show. "I think it will be attractive because of its content and its tone. On the other hand, it's a real flip of the coin as to whether people will be seeking that diversion. I know how I feel—I want to be at home. I don't want to turn to my work as solace. But all we need is two quarters of poor enrollment in our acting classes, and it all could go away."

She talks about a visit at Thanksgiving but hesitates. It would mean seeing Dad for the first time since the early 1980s.

That they have started speaking again is an event I can't fully account for. Some of it has to do with Dad's new-found security in Charlottesville, I suppose, his sense of being settled at last. I stopped trying to mediate years ago, but I have carried news between them when I had any.

Time-binder. That's one of my father's favorite nicknames for me.

A reunion between Meleesa and my father is a

fantasy I haven't risked having, and now we are talking about it as if it were simply a matter of making plans.

For my birthday dinner Ann makes roast cabbage, olive oil mashed potatoes, and lamb sausage. We drink a bottle of Ronco Nolé.

"This is the bottle of wine the thieves who broke into my car didn't steal," I tell her.

"It's a Merlot blend, from Friuli," Ann answers. "It's the only Merlot blend from Italy that's any good."

The *Post*'s lead editorial opened today with the phrase "No bombs have been dropped."

Charlottesville, Virginia
October 8, 2001

"The Taliban is already effectively gone," Senator Joseph Biden said this morning. Strikes have been directed at thirty targets. The plan is to send in CIA agents and commandos to fan out and find bin Laden. Ninety-four percent of Americans support the strikes.

Yesterday bin Laden appeared in a video in which he thanked God that the United States' "greatest buildings were destroyed." He described America as "full of fear, from its north to its south, its west to its east."

Marvin is now in our living room taking out windows. It was thirty-two for a low last night.

Dad and I have an appointment with a lender this morning. When Dad gets to the door, Marvin tells him a car bomb has gone off in D.C., although we hear nothing about this later on the news. The lender tells us we can drop our house payments about a hundred dollars a month. Closing costs will come to about $1,800, so it will take more than a year for any savings to kick in. We agree to sleep on it.

On the way home, we stop at Taiwan Gardens for eggplant and pork. I spend the afternoon reading chapters of a dissertation on Sam Shepard and his early years in Greenwich Village.

Anthrax has been found on the keyboard at the *Sun* tabloid offices in Florida. The two men who have been infected with anthrax are connected with the *Sun*.

Reid said yesterday that now we are all waiting for the other shoe to drop. "Because we know that they are not there—they're *here*."

Instead of yoga, Ann and I take a sweet nap. The room slowly darkens around us. Soon she—and the dog—are snoring. When she wakes up, we talk a little bit. A friend who called earlier said that her life will never be the same. There will be no freedom from fear.

I say, "I don't feel fear. I feel strung out; it registers as fatigue."

"What are you nervous about?"

"It's the realization, I think, that we've stirred all these feelings against us. That even though as a people we may be decent and good, our way of life inspires hate. To live with that—inside of that—is a huge loss. It's like a slave holder in the South who cherishes his way of life but who wakes up to the evils of slavery maybe a decade before the Civil War will blow it away and sees that he's got a wolf by the tail."

On the question of what is felt against us, the *New Yorker* quotes an Egyptian named Ali Salam. "These are people who are afraid of America, afraid of life itself. . . . These are people who are envious. To them, life is an unbearable burden. Modernism is the only way out. But modernism is frightening. It means we have to compete."

At 7:30 we meet Barney at the restaurant. B. P. O. Bernard Padien O'Meara. We roomed together at college for three years, and he attended both of my weddings. The first was to Libby Recknagel, in 1970, on the day after we graduated from Yale. The second was to Ann, in 1991, and was held about an hour north of Charlottesville, on Barney's Rappahannock County farm.

Since we grew up together, Barney and I have shared some powerful embarrassments. They are not things we talk about, but they are understood as a bond between us.

In June of 1969, in the summer before our senior year, Barney and I were invited to the Recknagel home in Upper Saddle River. I had been dating Libby for six months and had decided to stay close for the summer by finding a job in New Haven. Barney brought along his bag of tools and quickly fixed the solenoid valve on the family washing machine. Libby's mother cooed over him while I tried to make conversation with her father.

I was put to bed that night in Libby's room, with Libby on the living room couch and Barney on the screen porch. "We've got to get out of here," I said to Barney the next morning, before breakfast. He packed his tools and asked no questions.

During the night, as I lay awake in the child's maple bed, Libby had come into the room. We had just began to move together when her mother came to the door. "Oh, Libby," she whispered. For what felt like an hour we froze, locked in place. Then we got up and put on our clothes.

Her father met us in the living room in a rage. "How could you!" he bellowed. "And in my house!" We sat and took the anger; I had neither the wit nor the heart to say that they might be the intruders. At some point, I framed the words of an apology.

As soon as it was light, Barney and I left the house.

My task became to win her back. She did not need winning, but her fear of her parents had, I thought, to be overcome. In a car on the way to her house a few weeks later, I asked her to marry me. With her "yes," we quieted the resistance at home. Two months later, in another car, just before she dropped me at my bus at Fort Lee, I took the words back. "I can't do it," I said. The emotion had come over me like a breaking wave. I said it as she was pulling to a stop, at a place where cars whip by on the way to the George Washington Bridge. Back in New Haven, I called my parents and told them the wedding was off.

My mother sent Libby a letter:

Dear Libby,

Marry our boy! I like you so much, and I don't even know you.

We are confused because David hasn't been able to express himself over the phone, so we have no basis for understanding what his reason for postponing the wedding was. I hope that when we see him next week he will be able to explain himself.

A week later and a few minutes after landing in Reno, where I joined my family for a vacation in the mountains, I vomited out the window of my parents' car.

I was back in California. The Sierra Nevada has sustained me over half a lifetime, although visits there have been few in recent years. During those brilliant August weeks, it warmed me to the soul. I walked the familiar trails, soaked in the hot springs, ate the camp food around the smoky fire. My mother watched and said little; she never asked me to explain. She did urge me to talk with my father, who felt put at a distance. There is a photograph from that trip that does show Dad and me in the same frame. Perhaps it was the moment I opened up. We are sitting in bright light and hard shadows, on a slope at the end of some trail. Each of us sports long, thick sideburns, in the style of the day, as well as a week's worth of stubble. Our arms rest on our raised knees; we are both looking at our hands. I don't remember what we said, but it is true that by the time the vacation ended and I returned to school for my final year, I had resolved to win Libby back, and that I did.

So Barney has lived with me through all of that. He, also, never asks me to explain.

Barney was part of the best day of this year. Last June, Luke and I spent two weeks working together on the patio foundation, moving dirt and laying brick. Then, on Father's Day, Barney showed up at eight in the morning with a truck full of cedar poles he'd harvested from his fields. Some of the poles measured sixteen feet; the truck was riding on its axles. Barney's wife, Mary, and his son, Tim, were with him. The boys dug post holes while we laid out the arbor structure. Dad sat in a corner of the patio and kibitzed. It was like a barn-raising; the whole superstructure went up, magically, in a single day. Twelve hours later, we sat down to a huge penne and pesto dinner that Ann had made.

It's not a dish we've been able to make work at the restaurant. We ran across it in an *osteria* in Mantua, on a disastrous trip to Italy that left us swearing never to return. The waiter brought out a big plate with a raised rim. Piled in the center was a mound of pesto-laced penne mixed with sautéed green beans and grated parmigiano. The pasta rested on a creamy pool of potato purée. As we ate the dish, the purée worked its way into the pesto, softening and enriching it. Unfortunately, we found this summer that, among our customers, the audience for the dish, though fit, was few.

Tonight, as we eat our dinner, Barney admits to not

feeling much affected by the events of September 11 until this morning, when Tim and his girlfriend left the farm. "I didn't want them to go back to D.C. 'Don't drink anything but bottled water,' I thought. You can drive down Reservoir Road and not even slow down and do a hook shot into the city's water supply."

Barney helped build the Rappahannock County day care center and used to project movies at its one theater, in Little Washington. "The stuff in our county went on not as if nothing had happened but as if community was the most important thing," he says. "Mary and I talked about what we could do. And we both agreed that we could take people in."

Their farm of fifty acres is half pasture and half woods.

"I've always had a fantasy about the farm," I tell him, "in the event of nuclear war. I figure we'd show up with all the candy from the theater and hide out in your squash court. I could cook and tell stories."

"Well, all we'd need is wood, and we have plenty of that, for cooking and for heat. And there's lots of Canada geese around for food—they're like weeds."

That Barney so quickly adapts to my fantasy is a measure of his hospitality. His house on the hill is continually full of people; it's the most welcoming place I know. When I arrive, Barney simply folds me into the project of the day, whether it's transplanting white pines or hauling fieldstone. It is a comfort to have a friend who doesn't talk much and who simply expects me to work by his side.

Barney recalls the Thursday night Bush made his big speech. "It wasn't big on ideas, but it was perfectly delivered. In some ways, it may be a blessing that Gore didn't win. It has to do with the posture a president can assume in responding to a threat like this. Maybe only a Republican could do it."

There's a new joke going around, he tells us. Capture bin Laden. Give him a sex change operation. And then send him back to Afghanistan to live as a woman.

After Barney leaves, Ann says, "It's so reassuring to spend an evening with Barney. You have amazing male friends. Somehow, there wasn't a lot of envy stirred up."

"Well, when there was, people fell away."

"Still, you've been lucky. Most American men are like those dolls you play with in the bathtub. The fat ones, that you can just knock over."

◈

Charlottesville, Virginia
October 9, 2001

A first frost last night. Our house is full of holes from the construction and is cold this morning when I go upstairs.

Palestinians attacked their own security forces in the Gaza Strip for the first time yesterday.

The Afghan people consume eight thousand tons of wheat daily. Less than a week's worth of grain is now stored there. The United States continues to drop bombs and food—thirty-seven thousand rations yesterday. A thirty-ounce ration package contains no animal products so as to avoid running afoul of religious and cultural practices. It does contain peanut butter, strawberry jam, beans with tomato sauce, and potato vinaigrette. And a greeting: "This food is a gift from the United States of America."

Lots of windows go in today. The house was built without eaves or gutters, and after thirty years most of the sills have rotted out. The foreman comes by with a new contract. The windows, HVAC throughout, and the bedroom-bath addition will cost as much as Dad's house did a year ago.

"You know the latest casualty of the war?" Ann asks, when she comes home at four. "Our charcoal. Holly says it's been late all week." We burn about a bag a day; it's made in Canada from maple hardwood and shipped to us from South Attleboro.

We move downstairs, have a good time, and follow it up with a long, rambling discussion about the war. I find myself asserting the superiority of our way of life, its inevitable spread. It's odd to feel so partisan, after years or working to train myself to be inclusive and open minded.

Ann makes a veal stew with scraps from the chops that arrived this week. "I find now that everybody is gone, I can go back to Marcella without fear. It's simple—but what's too simple?" The stew has five ingredients: veal, pancetta, onion, garlic, and white wine. And a sixth—green olives. "The olives are the only modest flight of fancy," Marcella writes, "and they do no damage."

Last night Barney brought by a birthday CD. On it is one of those songs that you hear, love, and lose track of, Beth Nielson Chapman's "Sand and Water."

> All alone I came into this world
> And all alone I will surely die
> Solid stone is just sand and water, baby
> Sand and water and a million years gone by.

I suppose I truly believe that faith is not the strongest thing in the world. The strongest thing is looking at the way things are—we all will surely die, and there is no other world—and making the most of that.

I learn from *Newsweek* that the word "assassin" derives from *hashasin,* users of hashish.

◇

Charlottesville, Virginia
October 10, 2001

A British reporter, Yvonne Ridley, sneaked into Afghanistan on September 28. Wearing a *burqa,* she was quickly arrested and jailed. She made herself so difficult that her Taliban captors finally let her go. She demanded a lawyer. She demanded a doctor. A telephone. Writing paper. She was jailed for a few days with Christian aid workers who had been held for two months. Their cell, recently disinfected, had contained cockroaches, scorpions, and mice. Eventually she refused to eat. Ten days after her capture, she came out laughing, crossed back into Pakistan, and filed her story: "Freed from Taliban Hell."

When I wear my new sweat suit at breakfast, Ann says, "You don't look like a teddy bear. You look like a retired person."

On Monday, forty Taliban commanders, along with 1,200 of their men, switched sides and crossed over to the Northern Alliance, severing Taliban control of a major road in the northeast.

I spend the early afternoon at L'avventura making lamb sausage and unpacking wine and then come home to a mob scene. There are two guys in the living room and two hanging off the side of the house, trying to position a new three-paned window. The HVAC technician has ripped open an eight-foot-long carpeted bench and left the lid gaping like a coffin. The good news is, they've made progress on the bombe: we've insisted they chip away a little every day on Dad's birthday purchase.

Betty Fern calls from the department office at Maryland. One of my colleagues—three of us have been appointed to the promotion committee—has just handed her a section called "Scholarship." These pages and the report itself were completed—and needed to be completed—a week ago.

Around 4:30 the colleague calls. "Maybe there was a miscommunication or something, but I've written three more pages. Did you get my fax?"

"No."

"Well, I wonder if the report as it stands is strong enough. Maybe you'd like to qualify what you say."

"Do you mean qualify—or beef up?"

"Beef up."

"Fine. Go ahead and add whatever you'd like. Just clear it with Chuck." So it goes.

The anthrax that showed up in Florida is thought to have been stolen from a lab in Ames, Iowa. As many as five hundred labs in the United States store samples of anthrax. Iraq obtained two dozen strains of anthrax from one of our labs ten years ago. Stealing it is one thing; distributing it turns out to be more difficult. Anthrax spores in the environment can survive for decades.

A quiet evening at home for me. For the first time in a month, a sense of nothing to do. I watch *The West Wing* and *Law and Order*. They seem strangely shrunken.

◇

Charlottesville, Virginia
October 11, 2001

Today is Dine-Out-for-America Day. Ten percent of our proceeds will go to the relief effort. I will prep and cook tonight, while Ann runs the front of the house. We did only eighteen dinners last night, the worst showing in a month.

The men are at the house early, up on scaffolding, sawing out windows.

Bin Laden has provided around $100 million to the Taliban over the past five years. The CIA has concluded that he "owns and operates the Taliban." So far, he appears to be winning the propaganda war; the White House has persuaded the networks to stop airing al Qaeda statements live. They fear that the tapes may include hidden messages.

Madeline Albright appeared on Jay Leno last night, wearing a huge American flag pin. "My father used to say that when you go to most countries, they say, 'Welcome—so how long are you staying, and when are you going back?' Here, we say, 'Welcome, when are you going to become a citizen?'" When my grandfather Charles came over from Bohemia—where Albright's people were also from—before the Great War, he must have felt like that.

V. S. Naipaul wins the Nobel Prize today. Nobody writes any better about the second-rateness—the tacky imitative quality—of life as it is lived out in so much of the former colonial world. The Nobel committee describes him as a "Voltaire, who warns against all churches, all dogmas, all faiths that suppress reason and self-criticism." Naipaul quietly brings home the point that abuse does not justify bad behavior. Colonialism was a massive abuse by the first world of the third, and we in the West need continually to acknowledge that. We must do what we can. But are we, despite the grimness of the historical record, the legitimate targets of terror?

Home at eleven; too tired to write.

◇

Charlottesville, Virginia
October 12, 2001

Writing a journal, maintaining a vigil.

Too tired to write—I write. But I can't be. I've started carrying a three-by-five card in my pocket on which to jot down the things people say. I am living forward, now, with a beautifully desperate sense of time. If I look away for an interval—if I fail to record my daily quotient of words—I will slide into despond.

A huge evening at the restaurant last night, with seventy dinners. Donations will go to Windows on the World, the Trade Tower restaurant that lost more than seventy people.

We get hit hard and early. Many of the diners are new to us and don't get the implicit rules. Lots of no-shows. A party of six arrives half an hour late and expects to be seated. "It'll be fifteen minutes," Ann says. The woman in charge of the party walks out the door, then comes back and begins harassing Scott. "Put her party at table seven," Scott says. "I'll get those nice people I just seated to move." The woman is a bother all evening, demanding extra olive oil, fussing with her wine, and then asking Ann to remove $1.50 from the bill because her coffee was "too strong." This was her second cup; the first one had been "too weak."

"This was fucking Goldilocks," Ann says. "She even has the white dyed hair to be that person."

Around seven Ann pulls Dad over from the theater, where he has been selling tickets. "He's the perfect bus-boy," she says. "He spends just enough time with each customer to make him feel wanted."

We bake our own bread, a sourdough ciabatta using a starter made from wild grapes. But the wait staff habitually gives it away in huge quantities, to bridge the entrée gap, and we have a standing order to hold back. Later, Dad says, "I broke the rules. Anybody waiting, I pumped them bread."

In the kitchen, we're humming until twelve tickets go up at once. Then I forget to drop a rigatoni on a four-top. This puts the table at least ten minutes be-hind, with their other pasta orders already cooked and cooling. When I pull the already-late rigatoni out of the pasta boiler and throw it into the meat sauce and the béchamel, I see that it's underdone. So I pick out each piece, dump it in a colander, wash it off, and boil a small pot of water in which to finish it off. When the dish finally makes it out of the oven, I tell Scott to comp it.

This was not how I had planned to spend my fall. I had planned to write a memoir of growing up in south-ern California. I started outlining it at the Cape, two weeks before the planes hit.

I'm perfectly happy and utterly surprised to be doing another kind of writing, this daily journal-keeping that also eddies into the past. And I'm also more than willing to do what I can at L'avventura, to go out on a high note. There are days when I even feel a mysterious joy at the fact that my life has conferred upon me the roles of professor *and* chef. I have come to like living in two places and having two jobs. In either place, I can feel like a spy from another reality. Better than that is the sense that any identity assigned to me I can also exceed; what you see, in Charlottesville or College Park, is not all that you can get. In my bleaker moments, I worry that I am simply a master of compartmentalization.

Being a restaurateur is not a pill I've been forced to swallow; it's a choice I willingly made. It's not as if I didn't eventually get tenure and therefore had to go to work at L'avventura. But when I am seen there it's usually out front, as a host who also clears dishes. I'm a "server," to use the new nongender-specific word. On most nights I have no problem with the job—work is work, of whatever variety—but a few of my former colleagues at Virginia have a little trouble adjusting to my new role.

Or maybe the problem is mine. About two weeks after we opened, I was working the front of the house when a four-top came in. I recognized one of the men, a Virginia faculty member I'd met a couple of times at dinner parties. He looked through me; there was no hint of recognition. I seated the party at booth number four.

The man in the other couple ordered flank steak. Meanwhile, he began harassing Scott with little requests, like butter for his bread. Bread in Italy is never served with butter, I want to scream, and besides, we have already poured you a perfectly nice bowl of olive oil. Over the next half an hour, Scott keeps muttering and has me well stirred up. As I pass the table, the man looks at his steak, catches my eye, and says, "You should tell your chef that this is no good." In a quiver, I respond, "Most people like our food very much." Then I turn on my heel and walk away.

An errand takes me by the table five minutes later. As I'm passing, the man gets up and stops me in the aisle. "I didn't like the way you spoke to me," he says.

"Well, I didn't like the way you spoke to me."

"I have a right to point something out."

"I'll tell you something," I answer. "Most people find the food as good as we have found you a difficult customer."

He begins to turn red. Somewhere in the back of my mind I remember Ann telling me that he has a serious illness. The thought does not induce charity.

We are arguing in the middle of the aisle, within earshot of twenty diners. The man I know keeps his head firmly turned in the other direction. Finally I say, "Do you want to step outside?" At this he turns and sits down.

At the bar, I tell Ann what has happened and that I'm going out for a walk. She will apologize for me as

148

they leave, and, six months later, when they summon the nerve to come back, they will stop at the theater ticket window where she is working and ask, "Is your husband here?"

"Yes," she replies, "but it'll be all right."

At a memorial service at the Pentagon, yesterday, Bush said that "the loss was sudden and hard and permanent." Bombs in Afghanistan have devastated mountain cave complexes and may have struck the Taliban leader's Chevrolet Suburban. The huge pile of debris in New York is still hot; I-beams pulled out of it sometimes glow red.

I've just come across a new poem by Charles Wright. Charles lives across town on one of the old, tree-lined streets in the neighborhood where Luke was born. His imagination seems to operate as if fall were always in the air, and winter coming. A poet of our extinction. In this poem, he writes about driving our big roads—

> In southwest Virginia, just this side of Abingdon,
> The mountains begin to shoulder up,
> The dogwoods go red and leaf-darkened,
> And leftover wildflowers neon among the greens—
> Early October, and Appalachia dyes her hair . . .

—and about living out his days on our little local ones—

> On Locust Avenue the fall's fire
> Collapses across the lawn,

The trees bear up their ruin,
and everything nudges our lives toward the
coming ash.

In L'avventura's early days, Charles was a regular. Then he ordered an undercooked lobster and hasn't been back since. I'm a little astonished when I think of all the people in some way lost to us because of the restaurant business, the friendships untended, the customers here and gone, the employees sent packing.

Glamour. That's the word Ann won't hear of when it comes to the restaurant life. "There are five cook-books over there," she says one morning at breakfast, "and when you pick any one up it starts with a feeling of being oppressed by the dailiness of life and then finds its way to a little trattoria in Italy where it all changes. Food writers have this idea that eating is al-ways connected to some epiphany. But there's no glamour in the restaurant business. Like anything else, it's about showing up day after day."

My father said something to Ann this fall—he sees her as a fellow veteran of the small business wars—that got to the heart of how the restaurant has changed me, or brought me back to a world I had put aside. "David went to Yale and became a professor so as to avoid being self-employed and having his father's life. Then he gave up Luke so as to avoid having his father's life—the life I had after Joy was killed. Then he married somebody who *has* his father's life."

It's only half-true; the part about Luke is much more complicated than that, but it's true enough, a pretty savvy assessment of the way I've managed to reconnect with the anxieties and pleasures in working in a service industry with aspirations toward an art form.

Business is dead tonight. At six I arrive to host, but we're empty until seven. I leave to see *Training Day*. Walking out afterward, my depression is the worst in months; the movie has simply triggered my latent noonday demon. I've been off the medication since March, and it may be time to start up again.

◇

Charlottesville, Virginia
October 13, 2001

This morning, over coffee, Ann says, "I remember this Bette Davis film from the forties called *They Live among Us,* about the Nazis. People in Florida must be feeling that way."

The letter meant for Tom Brokaw that infected a female worker at NBC was postmarked from Florida. "Everyone's in the exact same boat," says the editor of the *National Enquirer.* "Everyone's on Cipro."

At Sardi's yesterday, the lunch crowd was quarantined for an hour because of an anthrax scare on an upper story of the building.

I'm wondering today about living in this new state

of mind. It is, first of all, obsessive. Turning attention to anything else feels digressive, inattentive. It's not fear, in my case—it's interest. Then there's the minor guilt that goes with owning up to that. A sense of cashing in on the whole thing, of almost looking forward to the next piece of big news. After half a day of no incoming, turning on the radio can feel like walking the plank. And yet that feels *good*.

Saturday morning. I'm on the computer when Ann comes over and begins smooching on me, playing with my hair. "See, aren't you glad you have a dog? Because if you didn't, you would get even more of this. All the rubbing and kissing. We'd have to cut your hair, though. I might even get you a retractable leash.—Now isn't this cheering you up?"

"Yes. It's so absurd."

"It's *not* absurd. It's just the way I play with Norma, and she loves it."

The grass in our yard has turned to weeds two feet high, and today I attack it with a weed whacker. It must be eighty degrees, and my protective goggles quickly fog up. A neighbor has his rain bird going, trying to eke out the last green of summer.

I call Bob Schultz. He's rushing off to a homecoming dinner but has time for a brief story. "I drove over to Davenport, for a book fair, last week. Lots of Iowa authors. At the end of the thing, everyone was heading out for dinner, and I was packing up to head home.

This young woman came through—dark, beautiful—and said, 'You're going to be late for supper.' 'Oh, I'm not going.' 'Are you one of the authors?' "Yes.' 'Well, I'm Miss Iowa.' We chatted a while, and then I said, 'Let me show you my novel. You might find it interesting—it's about men looking at women. It's called *The Madhouse Nudes*.' So I gave her a signed copy, and she gave me an autographed photo. She was really attractive and seemed like she was . . . a reader. Sally was waiting outside; we drove home immediately."

No one is more married than Bob and less susceptible to temptation. And no man I know likes to look at women more than Bob does.

A steady night at L'avventura, with fifty dinners. At 9:30, Barney, Mary, and Tim show up. I suggest chef's choice and bring them grilled shrimp, a veal chop, lamb sausage, and baked rockfish with tomato, capers, and olives. It turns out that Mary knew someone on the plane that hit the Pentagon.

"There's gonna be more," she says. She has been talking with a channeler.

Dad joins us, and we convince him to supervise George on Monday, when he cleans the kitchen. George doesn't have a key and tends to break things. Dad has just finished a long day of selling popcorn at the theater. He shrugs and says, "I don't make plans. I wait for the weather."

"One of the symptoms of what's going on," he goes

on to say, "is that people can't read the chalkboard." We list movies and times on a board just outside the box office. "I had a couple come in and out three times, before they figured out when the movie started."

Mary brings up an old canard. "Do you remember, Dave, the time you recommended a movie to me called *Body Double*? I rented it; the kids were nine and seven. I've never gotten over that." It's the De Palma film in which Melanie Griffith as a go-go dancer simulates sex to a song by Frankie Goes to Hollywood

"But look at Tim now," I say. "He turned out fine." Tim graduated from Yale last spring.

Mary's hard of hearing, and when Tim gets into it, she can't make out what he says.

"Yeah, Mom, wasn't that the one about 'pussy shaving'?"

"What?" Mary asks.

Tim hesitates, looks at all of us helplessly, then repeats the comment, in a lower voice.

"What?" She bends toward Barney.

"PUSSY SHAVING!"

The night goes like that. We agree that, this year, we'll have Thanksgiving on their farm. It looks like Meleesa and her family may come—at least that's the latest news—and Luke will also be there. Courtenay can't get away; she has to be in the medical intensive care unit. Ian will be staying in Pittsburgh.

If we can just make it to Thanksgiving, I think, we will be all right.

"Actually, the movie I was thinking of the other day was *Watch on the Rhine*," Ann says today. "Although I kind of like the sound of *They Live among Us*."

More news this morning about the first case of inhalation anthrax in this country since 1976.

So now it's cowardice by mail.

Ann this morning: "Every time we go into these places with caves and rocks, the rocks win, and we lose." She wants to see a bigger domestic crackdown, with lots of detentions; I argue that bombing is necessary, too.

A letter addressed to "Ann and Dave" sitting on the bar yesterday. From the fired hostess. Dad says don't open it; I agree. "I realize I shouldn't have said anything when I let her go," Ann says. "But I did, and gave her something to chew on. I should have just said, 'You haven't been supporting me, and that's it.'" Phil Halapin keeps a file of these letters—unopened—against the day when we might be silly enough to want to read them. Phil's mantra is "Denial of Access." If someone is causing you pain, break off contact. Withdraw and don't explain. Explanations are seductions. Or, as Dad likes to say, "Where there's drama, there's interest."

In the early afternoon, Bob Schultz calls back. We

talk about windows. They hired Andersen to remove thirty old sash windows without disturbing the interior molding, at a cost of sixteen thousand dollars. "You've got to write that big book," Sally says, when the issue of money spent comes up.

"That's what wives are for," I respond, "to remind us of all that we're not doing. I guess we'll have a nice home here, too, in about six months, just about the time we may be getting out of the restaurant business. But what will we do then, with all that space and time? Maybe we'll watch cable TV; all we get now is NBC."

Yes, Bob answers, "what's the content of that going to be—that habitation? It could be a mini-retirement."

"Maybe not. Ann's wavering about selling."

"It's only something you can feel your way through, I suppose."

"Well, at least we've taken control. We're working hard—Ann especially—and we've eliminated the 'energy sucks,' as Dad calls them." I tell Bob about the unopened letter.

"I guess there are people I avoid," he muses.

"Well, I have a colleague I don't speak to. I cut him off in a meeting, years ago, when I thought he was behaving badly. He wrote me a letter; I threw it away without reading it. And we haven't spoken since. I guess I've grown pretty ruthless about being only with people who make me stronger."

Courtenay calls. "I'm meeting the parents this week. Mom's a cellist, and Dad's a lawyer." Things with

Dan have been hard though, lately, since she's been on a rotation that leaves her no time. "I say things like 'Maybe I can see you on Saturday—maybe.' When I met Dan, I was on ambulatory and had all the time in the world. Now it's no more of the impromptu stuff. He's *learning*. But when I talked to Steve, he said, 'Get rid of him.'"

Steve is Courtenay's ex, a man she lived with for years and the one we thought might one day walk her down the aisle. He often loans her his car and still visits her in the city. I wonder aloud if it's not a little odd to still be in such close touch. "No, it's not," she says. "I'm not angry at him, I think he's a wonderful person, and I like spending time with him. Just because we used to date is no reason not to hang out."

She is wonderfully stubborn, I think, often at her own cost, and perhaps still half in love with a man who was easy for all of us to take. Steve and I were fond of each other and would exchange a nod whenever either mother or daughter began to spiral into an aria of complaint.

Rain today, the first in three weeks.

Dinner tonight with my oldest friends in town, Greg and Trisha Orr. Greg is a poet who teaches at the university; Trisha, a painter. He and I were hired by the English Department at Virginia in 1975. At the welcoming reception, Libby and I found the Orrs huddled in a corner of Bob Kellogg's screened porch, looking as uneasy as we felt. Then it turned out that Greg and I

had been assigned to the same office, and the friendship was born.

During the years when I knew him best, Greg was
at work on his third book of poems, *The Red House*. I
would one day publish an essay about this work and
Greg's attempt to write his way out of his story. At the
age of twelve, Greg accidentally killed his younger
brother, Peter, with a rifle:

> A father and his four sons
> run down a slope toward
> a deer they just killed.
> The father and two sons carry
> rifles. They laugh, jostle,
> and chatter together.
> A gun goes off,
> and the youngest brother
> falls to the ground.
> A boy with a rifle
> stands beside him, screaming.

Greg wrote about this moment in the present tense
because that was where it stayed for him. The event
stood at the center of things, surely. But there were
plenty of good times, at dinners at the Orr's rented
farmhouses or in our chairs tipped back at the end of
the day, gossiping or trading thoughts about the poems
that we loved, where we laughed and talked and never
thought about it.

The tenure decision came down in 1980. Greg was
given tenure, and I wasn't. We stayed close through the

years of my divorce. I met Ann, and we socialized as two couples. The break came in 1987, when I started teaching at Maryland and also had an affair. I drew Greg into it, and, when I broke it off and began patching up the life with Ann, I didn't have the courage or the imagination to bring Greg along.

So it's a friendship with years of silence in it. We began speaking again, in the mid-1990s, and are now close again. It turns out that Greg, too, has been working on a prose memoir, called *The Blessing,* and that it will be published in the coming fall.

For dinner on this October night, the Orrs have invited a prose writer newly arrived this fall, so we talk about where to get a hamburger in town, and how to avoid the summer heat, until the conversation turns serious.

It doesn't happen until we're halfway through the main course, a lovely chicken curry. Once the troubles come up, I can hear my voice rising with wine-warmed conviction. It's one of those conversations in which claim leads to claim until you find yourself way past the unclarity of your own position. "Modernity is like oobleck," I hear myself saying. "Once you touch it, there's no getting it off. Once the rumor that 'God is Dead' is out of the box, you can't recall it. These cultures are fighting a rear guard action against a cultural turn they cannot win." My tone grows querulous. My respondents stay calm. They express doubts about capitalism. The new guy says that he almost joined the anti-WTO demonstrations in Seattle. I can hear Ann coming to my defense, a sure sign that I've argued too far.

"You're a funny guy," Greg says to me. "I can remember when we first met, and you were dead set against the Vietnam War. At the same time, you couldn't get past this idea from Hemingway that a man wasn't a man until he'd gone to war. You were full of contradictions."

Then his tone turns a little somber. "But I shot my brother by accident when I was twelve. I've had a gun held to my head in Alabama. None of it holds any romance for me."

Accident. It's a word Greg and I think a lot about. "On the evening" of his brother's death, Greg has written, "several adults came to my room . . . and earnestly and compassionately informed me that it was an accident." But the twelve-year-old boy found that notion more terrifying than the idea that the event might have a meaning, a meaning he imposed by way of the story in which he became Cain and his brother Abel. He began to write poetry soon after. This work deals with the struggle to accept accidents *as* accidents, which is why it has so much appeal for me.

Because when my mother was killed, almost no one but myself wanted to see it as an accident. Some argued that she had been ready to go; she had completed her earthly development. Then there was the more troubling assumption that her life was becoming unmanageable, as was the that of the driver of the car, and that the two women had somehow chosen to leave. This belief had been reinforced by a stray remark, on the day of the crash, that the two bodies had been found "without a mark." It then became possible to believe that they had been translated, whole, to the other side.

The trouble was, I had seen the car, afterward, at the Texaco station where it had been towed. My mother had been riding on the passenger side, and the windshield on that side was cracked. And then there was the discovery, years later, of the death certificate. A handwritten note on the form described the cause of death as "massive injuries."

Accident. The root of the word comes from "cadere," as in cadence, as in the cadence of a poem. An accident is an event that does not fit into the cadence of a life.

Later on, Ann characterizes the evening at the Orrs' as "an exuberant superfluous discussion about how to fix things by well-meaning academics. I thought it was good that you finally laid your cards out there. My cards are that I don't want to do any bombing but I'm ready to abandon civil liberties. I wish I wasn't so changed in what I'm willing to do. In many ways, I'm glad I have this killer job. Maybe it will keep me in place."

◇

Monday morning.

"Ali Baba Café," John Auchard says, when he answers my phone call. He's sending his book—its current title is *After God*—to my agent in New York. Passages by everyone from D. H. Lawrence to Marilyn Monroe on the experience of belief in a secular age. "I write in my cover letter that the book was timely before the eleventh and might even be more so now. I really think that it's a useful thing."

John has a major Italian connection. "The scuttlebutt in Rome is that on Halloween, every shopping mall in the country is going to be hit and that this will destroy commerce."

We talk a little while about our emotions. I have more anger than fear. "To be frank with you," John says, "I don't know what I have. These emotions are so new. We now face war in a way we never did in the past. The big fear, of course, is smallpox. Another Italian told me that five terrorists have already taken the stuff and are gestating, getting ready to expose themselves on the subway. The problem is, these people hate us not for what we do but for what we are. When David Letterman came back on, after the attacks, he told one joke. 'Do you know why the Taliban hates us so much? Because they don't have cable.' And, in a way, it's true.

"On the other hand, in my travel class we've been

reading lots of books by travelers to the Middle East. At some point, they all ask the same question: What would it be like to spend the first twenty years of your life staring at the desert? Rather than at Macy's or television. Even if we could put ourselves across, we may find that they may want what we have to offer, but it may not be deeply appealing to them."

Chaos at the house this morning, with Marvin in the bedroom sawing out an AC unit, the electricians yelling commands, and Johnny dancing on the scaffolding. I have to get out, so I jump in the car and head west, toward the mountains.

At Afton I turn south on the Blue Ridge Parkway. I park about a mile below Humpback Rocks and begin walking east. Soon I'm on the Appalachian Trail, on a gentle up-and-down section I have hiked at least twenty times.

In this part of the Eastern forest, the woods are mostly oak. Usually the maples provide the brightest red, but this year, even the oaks are sanguinary. The season has tipped; from now until spring, the light will outpace the warmth. A full sun comes through the leaves. I realize that their color comes from their pigment, but, even more, on a day like this, from the light passing through them.

Why do we go to the woods? To get away, surely. But, of course, what we are left with is ourselves. Nature can't talk back, and that may be the often unadmitted point. So I'm left alone with my thoughts.

What scares me the most, these days, is the sense of my own blood rising. I felt it last night, at the Orrs'. In some moments all the intellectual work of the past forty years falls away, and I'm engulfed by a tribal rage. I've long been aware of the two at-odds voices in my head, the loud, dirty-joke-telling, woman-ogling, racial-stereotype-harboring voice and the still, small one that advocates liberty and justice for all. What used to feel like a manageable argument between the two has turned into an outright war.

Four or five people on the trail. At my rest stop, a view east across the Shenandoah Valley and north to Massanutten and Rockfish Gap. Hawks riding the thermals.

That evening, while Ann is fixing dinner, Dad calls. "Have you heard? I'm sitting here going crazy."

"About what?"

"Anthrax has hit ABC. And Tom Daschle. Is Luke OK?"

"I just talked to him. He's fine—he's on his way to work. He moves around in a part of the city that's not likely to get hit. But look, come on over. Sit with us for a while."

"No, I'm OK."

"No, I mean it. We have bread pudding."

"OK. Thank you."

As we eat our rockfish, Dad tells stories from his war, about learning how to fly.

◇

"Dan," Marvin yells this morning, about eight. "Dan—are you up?" He likes to call people by pet names, and "Dan" is the one he has chosen for me.

Marvin wants to talk about a closet that's getting smaller by the day.

It's going to be a hard rain. One hundred hazmat calls this week in Fairfax County alone. The victim of the ABC anthrax hit was the seven-month-old son of an employee. The offices of the Senate majority leader have also been quarantined, and abortion clinics are now being targeted with white-powder scares. A story this morning about an Afghan man jailed for sporting an insufficient beard; he spent a night in a cell with eighteen others being held on the same charge.

Dinner tonight with Howard at the Calvert Café; I've driven north for the promotion meeting.

"I'm not fit for human company," he begins. "I got into a huge fight with L. in the mailroom the other day, about Naipaul. She was going on about the choice being 'inappropriate.' I just couldn't help myself."

We are both happy about the choice—excited that they chose a *writer*. "He's Rushdie with a brain," I say.

"David, there is no piece of literature I have looked

forward to more than his Nobel acceptance speech. One of the best things he's said lately is, 'When religion organizes its storm clouds, I run for cover.'"

Howard is full of stories and quotations tonight. "I was talking with someone who has been editing Camus's late pieces. And she came across this wonderful sentence by him. 'My greatest fear is that history will become forensic.' I asked her, 'What's your sense of "forensic"?' And we both agreed that Camus meant the fear of a culture constantly digging through the rubble in order to piece together an indictment."

Then Howard remembers a story told to him by his mailman, after the poisoned letters began arriving. "'I woke up in the middle of the night,' he said to me, 'and I shouted out a word. "Carrier."'"

Forensic. Carrier. We are lost in a forest of double meanings.

In the usual talk about our marriages, I find myself saying this. "My experience is that change happened in response to demands. People change *for* other people."

"Well, I'm a little envious, I guess."

Then I see that he has misunderstood.

"Not *my* demands. I wasn't the one making them. I didn't have the courage for that. I may have acted out, and then that got through to Ann. But, no, it was my sense of the pressure of an ultimatum—coming from her—that got through to me."

Back at the apartment, I'm already in bed when Luke returns from his late shift. We chat a little about

The Lord of the Rings, which he is rereading. "He imagines an absolute evil," Luke says. "I'm no longer very interested or convinced by that."

◇

Charlottesville, Virginia
October 17, 2001

Up at 7:30 this morning. I shave and put on a coat and tie. As I'm going out the door, I tell Luke I'll be back around five, after the promotion meeting. "Is that why you're wearing that outfit? 'Let's be adults and make decisions.'"

Twenty staffers from Daschle's office have tested positive for anthrax. In the *Post* this morning, a "life-size" photo of a gatling gun shell being used in Afghanistan. It's the size of a banana.

I meet with Chuck Caramello, our chair, at 10:30. The report just handed me—the one a colleague insisted on fiddling with a week ago—is full of typos and grammatical errors. I ask Chuck to let me lead off the meeting, scheduled for today at noon, by apologizing for its quality. We agree to call it a work in progress.

A promotion meeting is the most serious occasion in the life of a department. By the time the meeting occurs, most of the snakes in the grass have been flushed out. This year, there are no snakes.

The candidate has six strong outside letters. He has no internal enemies. He's a great teacher and a founding figure of major organizations in his field. And he has produced what a colleague used to call "a book-like object." The book has been accepted by a university press, but it has not yet been published.

At one point during the meeting, the manuscript is said to "hold everything up to the fire of deconstruction to purge it of a whole lot of dross."

States of anxiety masking as intellectual concern. Whenever someone begins by saying "I'm concerned that . . . ," you know there's a red-hot poker headed up your ass. I've already asked the group to focus on the merits of the case and not on the status of the report. I haven't put my name to a document this messy in many years, but there's no point in giving my colleagues the back story. I find myself feeling calm. As the suggestions begin to mount, I bounce questions back. It's not until the end of the hour that I find myself aroused. I finally say this:

"I've sat on the university promotion committee. You read seven files a week—about chemists, agronomists, people in dance. All you come to care about are the outside letters. You notice the letterhead, and you look for the sentence that says 'Promote.' You don't have the time to get into the fine points of an essay written by the English department about one of its own."

It's not that I don't care about the report—I do. It's that after having written seven of them, I've developed a sense of the relative importance of the task involved.

And, while my anger at being turned back at Virginia has long since cooled, the memory of the damage done remains. Not that I have any ultimate regrets; my life, had I been promoted there, would not have become so rich and strange. Part of the shock had to do with the timing; three weeks after the official phone call, Libby came downstairs and said she wanted a divorce.

When the call came, I was cleaning up after a dinner party. Libby followed me into the study and watched me pick up the phone. "David," the voice on the line said, "this is Edgar Shannon." Libby stood at the end of the desk, in a flurry of restraint. "I'm sorry to have to convey this news," he went on. "The department met tonight to consider your case and voted against promotion." Involuntarily, my hand went out and my thumb went down. "I'd be happy to meet with you tomorrow to discuss this. Can we say my office, at ten o'clock?" I agreed, thanked him for calling, put the receiver down. Then I walked back in the kitchen to finish the dishes.

That fall, after the long hours in my library office, reading and writing alone—the department had given me a research leave—I had fallen into the habit of coming home and pouring myself a Scotch at the end of the day. I would take it into the living room and stretch out on our thick pile carpet. While I sipped it, I ate a bag of corn curls. Luke would come in and climb over me, his daddy Gulliver, and I would tickle him or not respond. I had kept the lid on and screwed it down tight. As I stood by the sink, scrubbing and rinsing, Libby danced around the kitchen, uncoiling like a spring. "Aren't you even going to get mad?" she yelled. "Aren't you even going to get mad?"

At ten the next morning, I walked into Wilson Hall and knocked on Shannon's door. He and Austin Quigley sat in two chairs facing me across the narrow office. As associate chair, Austin had the task of being there. It had been a few years since I had seen Austin socially, but the memories of our early, friendly years at Virginia, and especially of his scorn for the men who would judge him, sat there between us.

Edgar began by trying to explain the decision. Given the confidentiality of the process, there was little he could say. Moreover, he did not know my work and scarcely knew the department to which he had recently returned after serving fifteen years as president of the university. He seemed at a loss. Things got said about my book not being quite a book, about its internal contradictions, of the sense of it as a collection rather than a whole. I had tackled seven authors in a department committed to multivolume editions and biographies; they liked the long haul. The meal had not been thoroughly chewed; I had gobbled my food. Austin said little, but he had the courage to look at me. I asked a few questions, but there was only one thing, apart from all the reasons or thought of reasons, that I wanted to say.

"I consider it a personal betrayal," I said. Hearing that, I felt my anger rise. "You know me here—people know me, in this department. It's as if because you know and care that you can't let that count." I urged them both to see the matter as a personal thing. Something in me refused to admit that it all might be, for them, a technical affair. Austin said nothing, but I could feel him twisting on his spine, saw the water gathering above the lids. I bolted out of my chair, mumbled a good-bye, we shook hands, and I was out the door.

As I rounded the corner at a half-run, Irvin Ehrenpreis, who nurtured an odd affection for me, sprang from the doorway of his office. He had been waiting. He put out his arm to stop me. I pushed it aside and began running. I ran up the stairs and out of the building, past Randall Hall, and up to the first garden along the East Range. I got inside it. The garden was empty. At the center was a small space surrounded by ancient boxwoods. They billowed up, twice my height. The circle of green-black foliage blocked out any light, except where it came in from the sky. I stood in the circle and howled.

To this day I do not entirely know what happened. Five candidates came up for tenure that fall, two had already been promoted by the time they got to me— the fifth and final case—and the department had never before tenured more than two people in any one year. Wally Kerrigan called a few nights after the decision and said, "David, you got screwed." Ray Nelson walked straight into my office and said he was sorry. Alan

Howard stopped me on the stairs—we had exchanged words once in five years—to say that he admired my work. Word came back that, in the meeting, Hal Kolb had admired the power of my sentences. Steve Railton had given a last-ditch speech. Tenured the previous year, he had reached conclusions about fathers and sons similar to my own, but in a book about a single author, Fenimore Cooper. Jim Nohrnberg had made his plea. I had written a brief description of my second book, a work-in-progress about the literature of California, and had submitted drafts of two chapters. From a Central Valley family and raised in Berkeley, Jim had sense of the project's promise. "What a mistake," he said later, "not to have played the California card." He had held back, perhaps, out of deference to the department's parochialism. Culture stopped at the Shenandoah for most of the people in the room; they could not come with me across the wide Missouri.

The letters of condolence started coming in. My favorite was a handwritten note from a teacher at Yale whose course I had audited but to whom I had never been formally introduced:

Jan Something

Dear David—

We may as well use 1st names, since we are (in the grand Kabbalistic mixed trope) sparks of the same rust. It isn't lack of concern or sympathy that makes me answer so belatedly your kind note of Dec. 4. Perpetual family & personal crisis makes me nothing *but* belatedness. I'm writing to the good, gray Shannon a dossier letter for you once I finish scrawling this note.

What can I say for your comfort? You *know* that the profession is a deathly clerisy, and that the drab company of Herman the German, Ehrenberhen *et al* has *ausgewurft* you is a spiritual compliment, though an inconvenience. So—I will write Shannon now a *careful* letter (I am, alas, the kiss-of-death) but let me know if there is any pragmatic aid I can bring.

Yours—H. Bloom

The Shannon phone call had erased Libby's future as well as my own. She had not been, in the traditional sense, a faculty wife. When we entertained, we both cooked and cleaned up. In Charlottesville, she had pursued her own career; by the fall of 1980, she was teaching child development at a local community college. But she had followed me to Virginia in the first place, and she knew, once the tenure news was in, that to stay with me would mean moving again. She had invested her time and love in my success and had betrayed no more interest than had I in imagining life if I were to fail.

So, three weeks after the phone call, Libby came downstairs and asked for a divorce. It was December 9, 1980. She had spent the evening holed up in the bedroom with the phone, talking with a friend, and I could feel the desperation seeping under the door. To calm down, I had gone out for a walk and had found myself aimlessly circling the block. We were scheduled to fly to California in two days to spend Christmas with my father. She came downstairs, sat me down on the couch, and told me calmly what she wanted.

The timing did look bad, but the break had been looming for years, and she was the one with the gumption to know it. "No chemistry," she said sometime in the months ahead, during the endless to-and-fro of separation. It was as good an explanation for the failure of our marriage as any other. We had been married young, the day after I graduated from Yale, and we had but slightly known ourselves.

The next two years were the most frightening and exciting of my life. By the time Libby and I had separated for good, I had landed a decent job in Charlottesville and was about to meet Ann. Soon thereafter, Libby moved back to her home state of New Jersey, taking Luke away. It would be five more years before I was back on the tenure track, although only a year after being hired by Maryland I found myself both tenured and a full professor.

After the Maryland meeting ends, I spend the afternoon doing one last edit of the report with Betty Fern. Then I drive into the city for dinner with Luke. Along the way, I pick up John Auchard.

"A slight emergency this morning," he says. "That's why I missed the meeting. I had to withdraw five thousand dollars from the bank and give it to my neighbor. She was going to lose the house she's trying to buy unless she could come up with ten thousand dollars by noon."

Out on 18th Street the three of us find a little Indian place and have a nice meal.

On the drive home, NPR broadcasts a special with Judy Collins. She does a song about taking refuge in a diner during a Colorado blizzard, meeting a stranger, walking to his cabin for the night. She's been singing for more than forty years, and the mournful voice is still bright and clear.

◇

Charlottesville, Virginia
October 18, 2001

The *Post* headline this morning: "31 Exposed to Anthrax on Capitol Hill; House Shuts Down; Senate Offices Close."

We sleep in until the noise wakes us. Soon Marvin is in the loft to replace the last of the rotting windows. Thirty-five degrees this morning, one of the workmen says.

At breakfast, Ann and I compare the burns and cuts on our hands. "I'm going to drop the veal chop," she says. "When the rack comes in, I spend an hour cutting it and end up with pounds of extra meat. Let's go back to the grilled pork."

At the office yesterday, Howard slipped me five typed pages. The Post-It reads: "F S & G—new book proposal." The proposal opens by saying that "This is a novel that in alternating chapters takes place in 1979/1980 and in 1942. It is written in third-person. . . . "A

German U-boat sailor murdered near Peggy's Cove. There's a wonderfully concrete section titled HOW THE NOVEL BEGINS. "We are in a nicely appointed library at the end of a long hall. A *very private* auction is taking place. On the tripod next to the auctioneers is an exquisite painting." The working title of the novel is *What Is Left the Daughter*. The proposal is the best thing I've read in weeks.

After picking up some carpet samples—our carpeted stairs have been eviscerated by the HVAC work—Ann and I drive out for lunch to a roadside café. A sandwich of grilled tuna, cucumber, and wasabi. We've been hoping to recruit the young woman who cooks here for L'avventura's kitchen. She comes out to sit with us, and the good news is that the café closes for the month of January, when we'll need her. Back at the house, the foreman tells me our rubber roof has failed. "I could step right through it if I wasn't careful." Fix it, I tell him, and get me a price.

I ask Dad to come over to look at the carpet samples. His career as an interior decorator—three or four careers back by now—culminated in a contract to do one of the navy's tank carriers. The USS *San Bernardino*. He decided on a Western motif throughout and painted a Wells Fargo stagecoach mural on the wall of the officer's lounge. He even carpeted the bridge.

When he arrives, he makes the choice in a minute.

I'm trying to take a nap when the HVAC man yells, "Mr. Wyatt!" He wants me to position a vent. I doze until Tom Brokaw. It's all anthrax. Daschle says, "This could be anyone."

George the dishwasher has called in sick, and I'm the substitute. I vacuum the house and then head for the restaurant about eight. It's a steady night, but I have time for quick dinner with Dad. He's still in a reminiscent mood.

"At the end, after my father's stroke, in the late 1930s, I was left to take care of him. Mother and me. None of my brothers would help; they didn't respect the regime. I didn't even have a driver's license. He was so thin that his feet were shifting around inside his shoes. One day, he wanted to walk over to a baseball game. And then I had to go get him. Well, that was a struggle. He just didn't want to move. And he had an incredible will—especially when he was himself. If I get that way, just shoot me."

Ann has whipped turnips into the mashed potatoes tonight.

◇

Charlottesville, Virginia
October 19, 2001

Congress has never been closed before.

"On a day of autumn perfection," the *Post* writes, "the Capitol dome rose above abandoned offices and a neighborhood devoid of shuttling taxis, bustling restaurants and staffers in purposeful stride."

But this is not the headline. The headline reads: "Special Forces Open Ground Campaign."

Ann does not like the carpet sample I've picked out. We get into an "I do—I don't" exchange. "Why are you so grouchy?" she says.

"Maybe I need to go back on the medicine."

I've lived with depression for years. All my life, I suppose, although a name didn't get put to the case until my mid-forties. Stale, flat, and unprofitable—those were the words that circled through my head when I tried to characterize the pervasive mood. In 1994, I started taking Prozac. It worked pretty well—the irritability went way down—and there were no sexual side effects. But my range of emotion contracted, as it does for many people on the drug, to the middle of the scale. I couldn't cry. Missing that, I went off the medication last spring. Ever since the planes hit, I've felt as if I've lost a layer of skin. When I'm not mildly elated, I'm back to my old grouchy self.

Ann comes home at noon. "I bought the carpet."

"Which one?"

"The one you liked."

I'm cooking tonight. My prep includes wrapping pork loin in prosciutto, making a fig-arugula compote, toasting bread crumbs, washing greens, snapping beans, grating cheese, baking off the bread. Ann will work the front of the house.

Sixty-five dinners. Our biggest money night—two thousand dollars—since we came back from the beach.

At home, the new roof is almost done.

◇

We sleep through the early phone calls. At breakfast, Ann talks about her therapy session with Halapin yesterday.

"He said that this is a country in which no one is afraid. Then, all of a sudden, we're afraid of everything. 'You're probably well prepared for this,' he said to me. 'You're practiced in being afraid. And, because of that, you also know what not to be afraid of.'"

They also talked about the young. So many of his young patients, he told her, can't seem to find work. This inability goes directly to the feeling of living a life without a core. And the cure for that is not "Get a job." They need to find meaningful work, and either can't find it or don't know what it is. "I look at your father," Ann says, "and I see how smoothed out he has become, with all that we've asked him to do at the theater and the restaurant." I remember Dad saying to me, early on in his first year in Charlottesville, that his goal was to avoid a feeling of uselessness. He makes about seven hundred dollars a month, between the two places.

"All I worry about," Ann says, "is getting enough sleep."

Courtenay also phoned in to report that she had met Dan's parents. "Mom is very New York and turned out in a beautiful New York way." The big issue is age; she's thirty-one and he's twenty-four. "None of my friends can quite get it; there's a little too much high-school scrutiny."

Rangers are now on the ground in Afghanistan. The anthrax mailed to D.C., New York, and Florida appears to have come from the same source. The FBI is closing in on a blue mailbox in West Trenton.

Ann opens a letter from the IRS and explodes. They've been hounding us all summer about nonpayment of taxes, despite the fact that they cashed our check back in May. I've been dealing with it. Now they've confiscated our six-hundred-dollar tax rebate.

"These idiots! If you weren't so passive, none of this would have happened!"

"What do you mean—passive? I talked to someone in person and was assured that everything was OK. What more was I supposed to do?"

"Talking to someone on the phone is not 'in person.' And I never would have gotten my wine book back that you gave away if I hadn't tracked that guy down."

"But I called him and wrote him a letter. I even got the phone number that you used to get to him."

"But I had to do it—I had to get it back."

"I'm not passive—I don't like being called passive after cooking my ass off last night."

"You are passive—you are. You just don't see it."

I can feel my body getting warm, and the anger spills out." "Fuck you!" I yell. "Fuck you! I don't have to take this." I stalk downstairs to the bedroom.

I'm feeling trapped, suffocated, unappreciated. I throw a bunch of clothes into a bag. "I'm leaving," I say to myself. Then the thought crosses my mind that I have nothing to wear. Except for some dress trousers, I don't own a pair of pants without a hole in the crotch or the knee. This makes me hesitate.

I decide to finish packing, go upstairs, and say, "I'm going away for a while. We need some distance from each other."

"You know, I always talk about leaving, but I never do. And you're going to walk out, just like that."

"You have a car that works—the truck—don't you?"

"I don't care."

"I'll get charcoal and leave it at the restaurant," I say, as I walk out the door.

As I drive away, I start to feel the absurdity of my position. I buy the charcoal, drop it off, and drive home.

When I walk in the door, Ann come over and puts her arms around me.

"You're an idiot," I say.

"I am *not* an idiot. I just—oh, you know. This is about the time of year the trouble started between us, years ago."

"I know. But I don't think that's it. We're just—I'm just—tired."

I devote an hour to ripping out weeds and sawing down volunteer trees in my seriously overgrown yard. Ann leaves for the restaurant at two o'clock.

I spend the evening at home, alone, reading the script of Howard's new play, set in Churchill, Canada, hearing, every few minutes, the roar of the crowd from the Virginia football game with Florida State.

I realize when I finish the play how much of Howard's writing involves a woman, a bed, and a nearby fire.

The evening alone, under the lamplight, with the photograph album.

Home always breaks up after the mother goes. Especially when she is suddenly gone. Could she have held it together? Mother, my mother, where are you. . . . But these are questions of paradise.

As I lift up the album, I see that its spine is broken. I open it carefully, and a few untended photos fall out. In most of our albums the images are arranged in no particular order, with fifties black and white interspersed among nineties color. Ann says our approach to the past is "postmodern."

But this collection dates from the 1940s and looks like something Libby put together with some care during the early years of our marriage.

The first photo is of her face; she is wearing a nurse's uniform. A little blue cross has been painted on the starched white cap. The entire image has been

182

retouched. Red lipstick on the wide, full lips. A mouth, like mine, that stretches wide when it smiles. Highlights in the thick black hair, above the widow's peak. I hadn't remembered her jaw as being so full, or strong. She looks to the side, the brown eyes lifted up.

During the war, when my father was away in the army air corps, my mother entered nurses' training. It was the only time she worked out of the home until I was in junior high.

I turn the page. Here are three couples around a table—it must be a nightclub in Clovis, New Mexico. Two of the men in army khaki, my father and mother in the center. He looks straight at the camera, as handsome as Montgomery Clift. She smiles to herself. Drinks on the table, an ash tray. No one ever drank or smoked in our home.

And here she is, in a rare moment of joy, crouched with a snowball in her hand, ready to let fly at the figure bending in front of her. The photograph is dated 1951. Our early, happy years in the mountains. Her hair is piled up on top of her head.

I prefer the images from the years before my birth. My favorite is the one I published in *Five Fires,* my second book about California. It was taken in Lynwood, in 1945, the year after my parents were married.

Five people stand in the foreground, in a row. Behind them, a house of white stucco and a red tile roof, with a palm tree.

My grandmother Eva stands in the center. She has

her arms around her two sons, Bill on the left, Ralph James—my father—on the right. They hold their wives, Elinor and Alice Joy. The men wear their dress browns and air corps officer dress hats. Eva smiles, but only slightly, but the four young people, about to set out on the great adventure of California after the war, grin broadly, especially Alice Joy. Her coat is trimmed with a wide, leopard-skin collar.

Is it more or less accurate to say that, fifty-six years later, my father is of these five the only one left standing?

I am in awe, as always, before this image of stupid hope. How could they know, in this moment of setting out, what none of us can know—the way that life will take us by the throat? No regret—none at all—for faring forward, but a kind of stunned surprise at the cost of the journey, and of who was chosen to survive.

◇

Charlottesville, Virginia
October 21, 2001

Ruth comes by this morning for her usual Sunday visit. She tells a story about how the war has hit home.

"The guy at Rent-a-Wreck who picked me up on Tuesday said that their business was certainly down, because of fewer tourists. But not nearly as much, though, as it was for his seamstress. He takes his clothes to S & K. She told him she's only working in the mornings. When he got there, with some alterations, he asked her why. She pointed to her clothes rack. 'It's empty,' she said. 'It's never been empty before.'"

An editorial in the *Post* this morning argues that Islam never had an Enlightenment. It quotes an historian who points out that "Muslims make up one-fifth of the world's population, but in the 1990s they have been far more involved in intergroup violence than the people of any other civilization." I am drawn to such claims, and strangely comforted by them, although what good they can possibly accomplish is hard to say. We will not transform our enemies by arguing that we are more tolerant or less fractious than they are.

It's remarkable that I can pick up a book and be so quickly pinned down by it. Last night I began reading John LeCarré's *A Small Town in Germany*. The year is 1968. A man named Leo has absconded with secret files from the British embassy in Bonn. The agent sent to clean up the case asks a diplomat whether the defector was Roman Catholic. "My goodness," he answers. "What an awful thing to say. You really mustn't compartmentalize people like that, it won't do. Life just isn't made up of so many cowboys and so many Indians. . . . If *that's* what you think life is, you'd better defect yourself. . . . After all, that's what you object to in Leo, isn't it? He's gone and attached himself to some silly faith. God is dead. You can't have it both ways—that would be too medieval."

A long talk with Ann about the fight yesterday. "If you want out of the restaurant, just let me know," she says.

"No—that's not it. I mean, it does leave me tired out. But I've actually been enjoying it lately—the intensity—and especially seeing you so caught up in it. We just have different styles of response to the stress. I'd like a little less reactivity—and I'm sure the depression is hard to live with."

"Well, I have two available responses: ignore it, or get angry."

"I'd like something more in the middle."

"There is nothing in the middle."

"Why is that—Why can't you adjust your response?"

"That's the way it is. That's the way I am."

"But we've both changed over time. We have to keep to the possibility of change."

Phil Halapin says that men are passive and women are angry. It's another conversation that bears out the point. But we talk our way through it and so have a quiet afternoon.

Dinner with old friends, with almost a replay of the conversation last Sunday at the Orrs'. I'm asked, "Well, would you let Luke be drafted?" I answer by saying, "The decision isn't up to me. He's twenty-two. But would I try to stop him? No. I'm not a pacifist. I think this is a fight we have to fight."

◈

Charlottesville, Virginia
October 22, 2001

A postal worker in the District has come down with a serious case of anthrax. Action on the ground in Afghanistan is shifting toward Kabul. In Milan, in a bugged conversation, a terrorist speaks of "an extremely efficient liquid that suffocates people." He talks about placing it in cans of tomatoes.

Bob Schultz calls from Iowa. He's busy with scheduling his department's courses and with a daughter who wants to go to graduate school in philosophy. "I think it would be great," Lucy says, "to grow up and become a person like Cornel West."

I talk about being seriously depressed.

"Is it about the world situation?" Bob asks.

"No, I don't think so. It happened last fall, too, when I was on leave. Leaves can be . . . uneasy times."

"Well, if you and Ann have different views of the restaurant, and if you come home and the house is a mess, and outside in the broader world there's a sense of upset, there's just no resting place."

"And then there's been this beautiful fall weather — it's been ironically lovely."

He mentions the Yankee-Seattle game last night, which ended too late for this morning's papers. I ask who won.

"The Yankees did. In the bottom of the ninth. It was an amazing scene. They had an Irish tenor who

187

sang 'God Bless America.' Only someone like that could have pulled it off. And then a Sinatra rendition of 'New York, New York.' The camera panned across Giuliani and Paul McCartney. Wartime baseball."

After her bone density test, Ann comes home and says it would be nice to go for a hike. I make chicken and roasted vegetable sandwiches, she takes Norma over to Dad's, and, as the roofers renail the cap on the hip roof, we set out. An Indian summer day, with temperatures warm enough to make bread rise.

We drive down the parkway and take our usual walk, the one I took alone a week ago. Just past the lookout area, we find a fire pit of stones left by campers. It's soft, spongy ground, with little patches of grass and lots of leaf mold. We lie down with our heads propped on a log and doze off.

The sun is so hot that it wakes us. Then we share our lunch. We haven't come that far—maybe a mile—but it's clear that the hike is over for the day.

Ann wonders if there is any place this peaceful in Afghanistan.

"Maybe in the high mountains," I answer.

It's a day out of time. Back home, Ann feels exhausted and takes a nap: she was up until two last night paying bills. I make a dinner of sautéed spinach, mashed potatoes, and pork spareribs in garlic and white wine.

"Is Meleesa going to come for Thanksgiving?" Ann asks, while she's finishing up.

"I don't know. She'll regret it if she doesn't. And Dad dies."

"Wait until you see his kitchen. It is not the act of a dying man. The color is—very bright. He even painted the *refrigerator*."

◇

Charlottesville, Virginia
October 23, 2001

It now appears that anthrax exposure in the District was caused by spores inhaled from the *outside* of a letter. Two D.C. postal workers have died, and two more are very ill. The major mail processing center in the city is closed. A Manhattan postal worker is quoted as saying, "We have letters that shred completely, and there's no test to tell what you're breathing."

The sheetrock has arrived. "Them boys is goin' to catch hell," Marvin says, "trying to get that damn stuff down your hill."

Seven pounds of veal stew meat awaits me at the restaurant. I'm making a big batch for a busy week; the film festival sponsored by the university starts Thursday and always brings in heavy business. Soak the veal pieces in red wine. Dredge in flour, salt, and paprika, and brown in oil and butter. Brown Italian sausage. Sauté onions, leeks, mushrooms. Blacken red and yellow papers over the gas flame; peel and slice. Cut up and throw in some carrots. Fry a little garlic; pour over a few cups of tomatoes. Add some lemon juice. Pour in the leftover red wine, along with a little white. Then the two secret ingredients: Dijon mustard and cognac. Stir; bake at 350 for an hour and a half.

I've forgotten the paprika, so Dad drives me home to get it. "I can't believe what you did to me," he says. "You gave me that book. And now I can't put it down."

He's reading *The Human Stain*.

"Roth writes so well about age. And living alone. There's also less pornography in this one. Although there's nothing wrong with pornography—who isn't curious about what the other guy looks like? We just don't love our animal side enough."

At the house, there is a man cutting window trim, one nailing shingles, another running duct work, and Marvin in the living room, tearing up carpet.

At 3:15 I pop my stew in the oven and walk a few blocks to my monthly massage. I have the usual side ache, and Beth works on it. "Can you feel it?" I ask.

"Oh yeah. It's probably from muscle tension. If you hold tight long enough, they sort of glue together, and it's pretty hard to break them down."

I head home around five to begin painting windows. Between the new ones and the replacements, I have twenty-six to prime and finish. When I first met Ann, I had just completed my seven years at Virginia and had spent the summer painting houses. Dad got me started painting early and has promised to lend a hand.

The photographer Joel Meyerowitz is on the radio, talking about his work at ground zero, where he's been taking pictures every day since the first week after the attacks. The most striking thing about the site, when he first gained access to it, he remembers, was all the sharp objects, the shards of metal, the possibility of being cut. "The ground was like walking through a field of swords."

Ann comes home, and we jump in the tub, with tequila and Triscuits. Afterward, we share leftovers for dinner. There's an Agnes Varda documentary showing on campus, so we drive over.

It's called *The Gleaners*. Varda drives around France with her camera, photographing people who roam through potato fields and apple orchards, after the harvest, gleaning the remnant fruit. She finds people who live entirely off trash, and people who make art out of it. In an abandoned vineyard, a family sings as it cuts down the grapes. One man, with a master's in biology, gets all of his food from the produce discarded when the market shuts down in the town square. He lives in a hostel and spends his evenings teaching French to immigrants from Mali. Varda's France is rainy and flat, with tough, eloquent people and little pretense. It's a world so layered and cultivated by human touch that people survive well and even happily there on mere gleanings.

◈

The news is bad this morning. You think you can rise above it, go about your little life. But today, for the first time, I feel a sense of doom. A sense of something unending in the air. The mail has been turned into poison.

In the District, the Postal Service sanitizes its trucks and orders anthrax detection equipment. The bacteria have been found on sorting equipment that handles packages for the White House. The main postal facility in the District is closed, and D.C. officials are preparing to deliver antibiotics to the general population. Luke has a mailbox in the city.

"Given that enough spores were present at Brentwood to infect four workers with the most serious kind of the disease," the *Post* writes, "spores could conceivably also have passed through the facility, winding up in the houses and businesses of Washington."

During our breakfast of waffles, Marvin is continuously running the air compressor. "I thought that thing only ran part of the time."

"No, if you're enjoying yourself," Marvin says, "having breakfast or something—*then* it kicks on."

"For the first time anyone can remember," the *Post* reports, "the Israelis and Palestinians are fighting inside the town of Bethlehem." *How still we see thee lie.*

I'm beginning to paint baseboard when Howard calls.

"David, I went out last week—a little literary evening—and it was a ghost town. Some NPR people, Jackie Lydon, Renée Montaigne. These savvy women; they're protected by the nature of their work against exaggeration. So it was interesting to understand the way they are looking at it from their various viewpoints—Brooklyn, L.A., the Middle East. I didn't sleep a wink."

"They just feel that D.C. has a certain inevitability about it. The president and the Congress are here. I drove back through the empty streets of the capital with these guys standing on the corners with their guns and their binoculars. And I thought: this is not Hollywood.

"It made me go in and stare at my sleeping kid."

The talk turns to life at home. "Ann and I have been fighting two or three times a week," I tell him. "It's as if we have nothing left, so the old grievances can come out. I even packed a bag the other day."

"The deep part," Howard says. "You don't want to cast your net there. Jane and I—I think we realize we're just agitated. It's been a strange time. We're just sort of side by side. I can't figure out what's really going on. Maybe we're trying so hard to keep the anxieties out of the house that it's announcing them in some ways."

"The old selves," I mutter.

"We went for a walk, the other day. There's a nice big house nearby—you know we've been thinking about moving. But I don't want to talk about a new house as a way of clearing the air in the one we live in.

Jane says she's feeling lonely. 'If you're lonely for me,' I tell her, 'you'd get that fucking TV out of the bedroom.' Silence. I don't know what to make of that."

"In my first marriage," I answer, "I complained a lot about being lonely. I learned later on that for me it was a code word for being depressed. Not that it's any great thing to know that, unless you can find a way to get help for it."

"One of the things Jane can do to contribute to not being lonely is to come to me, wherever I am in the house. I mean, I don't go out to bars. I'm *locatable*."

I laugh at the word. "Well, she's lucky there. Ann's always been locatable, too—even when things have been pretty bad. Somebody has to be, or you grind to a halt. I've always been grateful for that."

"What's going on in the world," Howard says, "is a shared experience, but if you hoard it separately, it's no good. The demarcation may really be September 11. Before then, we'd gotten back to something. Our meals together were so much fun. And then it happened, and the TV went back in the bedroom. I mean, if you wait till you're sixty, civility replaces everything."

We agree to talk again in the morning about our writing projects.

I'm painting a piece of shell molding when Bob Schultz calls. "I'm in a phone mode," he says. "Sally and Schuyler are away, and I've just read an Alice Munro story that I had to talk about. It's called 'Comfort.'

There are so many ways it could have gone wrong or been a little dumber in somebody else's hands."

"That's the one where the wife scatters the husband's ashes, at the end. It *was* good. I remember thinking: this story was inevitable—but not until it was written."

"I read something from a set of course offerings from Provincetown in which Michael Cunningham said that all we want fiction to do is to approximate the intensity of the most ordinary hour of our daily lives."

"Yup. Here, daily life is up and down. It's pretty turbulent. We have these great moments, and then there are long stretches of exhaustion and irritation."

"Sally feels like her energy's down. She's going to talk to somebody. She feels as if she's on the edge of it."

"Depression or middle age?"

We talk about whether or not to take a pill. Bob states his view: "If you need to take one—take one, I say."

"Sure—but you've always struggled with it. The anxiety." When I first met Bob, in 1981, we had desk jobs and would rather have been teaching. It took me a while to realize that under his angelic smoothness there was a self that felt, as he said, "made out of glass." He came with Iowa roots and a quiet kindness, but, driving up Route 29, his heart could begin to beat so violently that he'd have to pull off the road. After his return to the Middle West, the panic attacks began to

diminish, and he now controls them mostly with med-
itation and trout fishing.

Lately, though, Bob has been experiencing a new
manifestation of anxiety, a tightening of the throat to
where he can't eat or even swallow. It happened one
night at dinner this summer at the Cape, during our
annual reunion.

"You haven't wanted to be on a pill forever," I say to
him.

"Like I say," Bob answers, "when I feel like taking
one, I take one."

"Well, I may go back on something. Zoloft. Celexa.
The problem is living with a sense of there being something out there that will help you. And then not being
sure what it is. And then getting in a position to start.
It's a complicated thing. When you're on something,
there's always a yearning for weaning."

"I guess we all have these cycles. The trick is not to
think of any point in the cycle as 'the real me.'"

We talk about the terrorists. If they want to make
people truly afraid, Bob says, they could make somebody sick in a little rural town. "Here, we still feel as if
it's the East Coast, the capitals. I do find myself being
slightly more aware of it when I open the mail."

Bob, like Howard, wonders how much the larger
threat plays into our domestic lives.

"If you're starting the midlife change, it's pretty intense," I say. "Ann has been on and off estrogen a number of times."

"Well, there is a sense of diminishment that you hunker against. But it's such an old story, you feel silly. With us, it's all tied to a cycle; there's one good week every month. It sort of depersonalizes it all." Bob talks about a Buddhist notion of a calm that descends once one passes beyond the demands of being a husband.

"That's fine for seventy-five, although my Dad was still in a hot romance at that very age. But it's not acceptable in your fifties. Some days I think, 'I've got twenty more years of erections, and I don't want to waste them.' I can't believe that desire dies for anyone. I do believe that people can kill it off. When I look around, and I look inside, I think that the hardest thing is to go on wanting things, since—so often—we don't get them. With sex, Ann and I have taken to making appointments. A little formality, a sense of expectation and occasion—it seems to help."

"We make appointments—and then we don't keep them."

"That happens to us, too. Last week, we climbed into bed and then both fell asleep. But, at least we showed up."

It's the last warm night of the year—I believe—so I open the patio and work it until a little after eight. My veal stew has turned out well; Dad signals me, with a big smile while I'm taking an order, that he enjoyed his portion.

◇

197

Meleesa is coming for Thanksgiving.

This is huge news. She and my father have not seen each other since 1983.

At school yesterday, Howard tells me this morning, he went in to see the woman who runs the department's business office. "And she was weepy, and clutching her cross, and saying 'We must all love and be kind to each other.' And I looked around, at our colleagues standing nearby, and they all froze, in George Segal–like poses. I thought, 'I'm in the Arctic.' So much fear of letting emotion in."

"An epistolary novel has a curious structure," I say, when he tells me that's the form he wants his next novel partly to take. "Each letter has that limited horizon; it can't see beyond itself to the shape of the story. A letter doesn't look past its day." It turns out that a sense of being marooned in the present is pretty much the effect he's looking for.

After painting one window, I drive to work to bring Ann a sandwich. It's the first windy day, and the air is filled with leaves. Luke calls to say he's coming down for the film festival, so I have a big cleaning job ahead. The only room with a spare bed is full of boxes, moved out of the crawl space to make way for Marvin and his gang.

The boxes bear labels like "Courtenay's Books," "Time-Life Civil War Series," and "Ian's Sports Illus- trateds." Leavings in the empty nest. And all this stuff was somehow crammed into the tiny bedroom the two of them shared until Ian went off to college, fifteen falls ago.

When do you finally throw out your children's things?

Courtenay left two years after Ian did. It's hard to believe they're both now over thirty. Coco was in the seventh grade when I came along. We had six good years together, in the then-two-bedroom house that we are now expanding for the second time. With Ian, I had only four years, but they mattered less, since he was too old to look to me as any kind of father.

Dinner was our only ceremony. By five I was home—I was then working at a nearby foundation— and beginning to cook. Courtenay might be at the table, drawing one of the curvaceous, idealized female figures with full lips she was partial to. Just before the meal was ready, or just after, Ian would burst in, hot and sweaty from soccer practice. Ann would drive back from selling tickets at the theater, and we would eat.

It was a life lived around a circular table, and some- times the energy ran so high that I felt flung into a cen- trifuge, like the tigers chasing Sambo around his tree, running so fast that they turn into butter. That the kids both played trumpet only augmented the running

Laurel and Hardy routines. They did persiflage, Ann played straight man, and I threw in an occasional quip. When the table began to shake and the kids wrestled with each other and the dog, I would yell out from my hoard of strictures. The favorites were "Somebody's going to burst out bawling" and "No more treats!"

I liked being a stepparent, and I got pretty good at it. Caregiving without the ultimate responsibility. The buck stops . . . there.

There is a strong memory of the day on which the experience peaked, at least with Ian. It was the August before I began teaching at Maryland, and before the seductions of the new job drew me into an affair that almost blew our family apart. Something happened on that trip west with Ian that could not have happened later, given the damage I was so soon to inflict and given the inevitable attrition of the years.

By the summer of 1987, my family of origin had split into big pieces. My oldest sister, Megan, I had not seen since a quarrel at Christmas dinner in 1982. At twenty-two, the youngest sister, Madeline, still lived at home with Dad and Richard, although Richard would be gone by the next spring. Meleesa, the middle sister, had fallen out with Dad over recriminations about the past.

So, instead of arriving with my father and my sisters and my son, only four of us from Meleesa's side—Ann, Ian, Courtenay, and myself—showed up for her Seattle wedding. We were functioning well and united in the purpose of making sure she had a good time. We shared a condo on Lake Washington with two old friends and their two kids and spent the week canoeing, going to baseball games, ferrying through the San Juans. A day or so after the ceremony, we found a Lebanese restaurant and had a meal of two whole clay-baked chickens. The meat was so tender we carved it with spoons. Over rice pudding, we agreed to see the new Kevin Costner film, *No Way Out*. I settled the bill while the others started for the car. As I came out of the restaurant, Ian stopped me near the door.

He had been away at college for a year. That summer, he had lived with us again in Charlottesville, working at Arby's and taking classes at the university.

Ian clearly had something to say. He stood directly in front of me and fixed his eyes on mine.

"I just wanted to tell you," he began, "how much I—."

My mind reeled as he moved through the sentence. I had no idea of what was coming. Ian and I had a decent rapport; we did riffs at meals on each other's jokes, talked about sports, argued over movies. We did not talk about private things. I avoided demands that might lead to conflict, and he made way, in the house, for me.

"I just wanted to tell you how much I respect you. I mean it—I've been thinking about it all week, and I really want to say this to you."

I felt myself freeze, wince, relax a little. What was happening to me was a wonderful thing, if I could take it.

He went on. "I really admire what you've done for your sister. This has been a very nice week. The wedding was great—of course she deserves it—and everybody had a good time. I don't understand what's going on with your father. I can't imagine not being at my daughter's wedding. But you came through for her."

I muttered something, a "Thank you" or "I'm glad you feel that way."

Ian held me in the power of his words. He was giving, giving. I should have been able to accept what was being given; praise was my meat and drink. But there was the danger that I might have to respond in kind. We had already had our evening's feast, and now he wanted to follow it with more. He was feeling the power and passion of the man who gives everything away.

"I mean it." Ian leaned toward me. "Just the way you've done things—with Courtenay and me—I want to tell you that I respect that. And Mommy looks happy. I think you've made her happy. You know she had a hard time there, for years. She used to cry a lot on the couch. Now she looks good. I wanted to thank you for that."

The other six were out of sight. I felt welded to the spot. I tried to keep my eyes on Ian's eyes. Something in mine must have made him feel that he had to say more.

"I know it wasn't easy—coming into the house and having to fit in. At first I wasn't too happy about it. I mean, the three of us had been a unit, and we got along well. But it has worked out, and you were a part of it. Well, a big part of it, I mean—the new part. I'm glad that you came along."

"Thank you," I said. "I don't know what to say."

Ian started to begin again; there was no easy way to step out of the moment he had built between us. Then he looked hard, perhaps saw in my eyes the look of appeal. He held out his hand and I shook it, and then he walked quickly in the direction of the car.

◇

Charlottesville, Virginia
October 26, 2001

"Va. Case Alters Anthrax Equation." A mail worker in Sterling has been stricken. Somehow this complicates the mystery. "One possible explanation for the perplexing case is that there are multiple letters filled with tiny but potentially deadly doses of spores now traveling through the mail." Authorities face the prospect that the entire mail stream could be deadly. Anthrax hoaxes involving Nesquick and crushed pills are rampant.

"Your father is resourceful," Ann says. "When we ran out of coffee last night, he took a bottle of instant espresso and blended it with cold coffee. Scott, meanwhile, was going crazy."

At ten last night we watched Bergman's *Persona*. I had never seen it. The stage actress Liv Ullman gets sick and stops speaking. Bibi Andersen, as her nurse, takes care of her. "In 1966," Ann says, "it would have been full of symbolism." Back then, we would have worried the question of appearance and reality. Now, it seems a story about the power of withholding in a relationship. The longer Ullman is silent, the more Andersen talks and comes forth. In bed this morning, I said to Ann, "It seemed like a movie about our marriage." Fortunately, she laughed.

At 9:40 I'm sitting in Phil Halapin's waiting room. I read a poem called "Golden State." A California life, a father out of bounds. Not my story. But close enough.

Phil prescribes Effexor. "It's used a lot with older people. It works as a stimulant; sometimes the brain just gets tired. You may get sick—kind of a green feeling. That will happen right away. If it works, it will take hold in about three weeks."

At the house, Johnny is nailing shingles around our bedroom windows, so I go over to Dad's to take a nap. When I get up, he fixes me a lunch of tomato soup and grilled cheese. "You know what this is, don't you? Our first meal. When your mother and I got off the train in New Mexico, after the honeymoon, we invited a few other guys in the service over for dinner. Once we got to the store, she said, 'I don't know how to cook.' 'Well, I do,' I said, and this is what we had."

At two o'clock I arrive at the restaurant. We already

have sixty reservations; it's Parents' Weekend *and* the film festival. Ann makes an apple-rosemary tarte tatin, while I ready my station. It's a small kitchen with only two stations: grill and sauté. I'm sauté; Howard is grill. He is responsible for the pizza, shrimp, trout, lamb sausage, and veal chop. He also makes the romaine salads. I do the four pastas and the soup, cheese tray, roast grouper, prosciutto and figs. It's my job to run the line—to sequence the orders—and to make sure that the food comes out quickly and comes out hot.

"Lots of farmers out there," Scott says at six, about the early crowd. Parents with children don't tend to drink and often don't even know how to carry on a conversation. Working as the hostess, Ann grumbles about a run of no-shows. She starts seating walk-ins, and then at 8:30 we are suddenly jammed. Bill comes back holding two blank strips of white paper. "Do you know anything about the credit card machine?" he asks. It's running paper though without printing anything. It turns out that I've bought ordinary adding machine tape; the machine runs on thermal paper. Ann gets out the old slide-and-release imprinter and wrestles with it all night.

It's a big night; we sell four bottles of Brunello. The take is more than $2,200, our biggest night so far this fall.

I'm home by 11:30, and Luke still hasn't shown up. It's good to think that he's so busy with his life in D.C. that he got waylaid into staying.

◇

Charlottesville, Virginia
October 27, 2001

"Well, it's a weight-loss program," Ann says this morning, before going out the door. She means running the restaurant. "I want to get down to a size twelve so I can wear my Calvin Klein jeans." She's off to do concessions for a film festival movie, which she then hopes to watch. *Morocco*.

The Supreme Court closed on Friday for the first time in sixty-six years due to anthrax fears. Spores were found in an air filter at the Supreme Court warehouse. "Nobody believes the anthrax scare we are going through is the next wave of terrorism," a government official says. The threat is deemed to be "domestic."

So what do we do with this fear? It's easier to manage when it's compounded with hate, or disdain. I can hate bin Laden. But this free-floating enemy—these domestic nobodies—what do our emotions do with them?

Ann thinks George the dishwasher has had a stroke. He says it's a bad allergy, with swelling in the head. But his face looks twisted, and one side is paralyzed. He can barely speak or hear, and he breaks a bowl and a wine glass tonight. At staff meal, afterward, he seems unable to chew a very tender veal stew and does not finish his meal.

Later—weeks later—Courtenay will calm our fears

by guessing that George has a manageable case of Bell's palsy, a diagnosis confirmed by an attending at the university ER.

Friday and Saturday this week are days lost to the restaurant business. I say "lost" because of the peculiar way this work has of absorbing all your energy and leaving you without any tangible residue of accomplishment. Of course, appetites have been appeased, but they regenerate, and money is made, enough to cover costs. The pleasure is in keeping the machine running and in fulfilling our vision of what food should be like: simple, fresh, affordable. Or, as my insurance agent says, "The point is to have an identity and to pay the bills."

By 7:30 a weekend evening takes on a hum. It can be a swirl of pleasing effort or hysteria. On Fridays, customers spend less time and less money. They are in a hurry to grab a big night, still wound up from the week. They order more pizza and drink less wine. Tips are down, sometimes even forgotten.

Saturdays take on a mellower tone. The people who drift in are willing to wait. Regulars arrive in pairs of pairs; this is the magic number, the foursome that fills a booth and makes for good conversation among old friends. The house warms with a generous mood; on a night like tonight, people order starters and desserts. If I'm working up front, as I did every weekend during our first four years, I turn the music up, the lights down, and think about what a marvel of culture the weekend is.

We do eighty-four dinners tonight, run out of everything, and are thawing trout at 9:30.

◇

It's Sunday morning and we plan to sleep in, with an hour gained from the clock being set back. But around eight we hear the sound of hammering. "What's that?" Ann asks. "Is someone working on our house?" No—it's the neighbors. We talk a while—"I'm actually having fun," Ann says, about cooking. We had a good week, with six thousand dollars in receipts. The hammering goes on.

"It *is* our house," Ann yells, when she goes upstairs. There, at the front door, is Marvin, finishing the front deck. "I took some time off last week," he says, "to see a friend in the hospital. So I'm making it up today."

The CIA will now be authorized to assassinate not only terrorists but their financiers. "You can make the case that getting the funding people would have a tremendously chilling effect," an inspector general argues, given the fact that such people are not commonly prepared to die for their cause. A problem with the plan is that the CIA appears to have lost touch with the brass-knuckle types who actually go out and kill people.

An article on the cost of the attacks estimates that the Pentagon sustained one billion dollars in damage, while New York property losses are estimated at thirty-four billion. The amount of office space lost in New York alone equals the total office space in Miami or Atlanta. Renaissance Cruises has filed for bankruptcy. As has Vectour, the nation's largest bus tour operator. Visits to the Bronx Zoo and the Museum of Modern Art dropped 47 percent in September. The "lost human productive value"—the salaries that would have been earned, over the years, by the people who were killed in New York, is estimated by the city's comptroller at eleven billion dollars.

The price of things. It's a phrase from Joan Didion that is never far from my thoughts. And it actually plays a part in the story of how Ann and I met.

It was the fall of 1982. The phone rang one day in the foundation office where I had landed a job after leaving Virginia. A voice on the line said, "This is Ann Porotti." I said hello. Then she said, "Are you ever free for dinner?" I paused, then said "Sure." "How about Thursday night?" I agreed and also agreed to drive.

Ann and I were acquaintances in the way of small-town life: the passing nod on the street, the greeting in the lobby, the absence of any formal introduction. She was often visible standing in the Market Street window of the movie theater she owned and managed. The first time we had exchanged more than a few words had been at a dancing party held a week before at the big house Al Filreis and I had recently rented together; that June, Libby and I had separated for good.

On Thursday night, I put on the new brown jacket and tie that Dad had bought for me on a trip home to California and drove across town to the house on Rothery Road. My knock on the door was answered by a twelve-year-old girl. "Hi. Mommy's not home—she's at the theater. Come on in." Courtenay kept up an easy patter until Ann arrived, twenty minutes later. We chatted about her father, Chief, who liked running the bar at Fellini's, the restaurant he and Ann had opened a few years earlier. Ann rushed in, changed quickly, and we set out in my car.

I can remember that evening as if it were yesterday.

She took me to Eastern Standard, Charlottesville's first stab at nouvelle cuisine. I did not know that she had already downed two cognacs while trying to calm the girlfriend of the man she had just fired. I did not know that she was allergic to scallops, which I promptly ordered. I did know that she looked good across the table, all five feet two inches of her, with the small, full mouth and the wide smile, the jet-black hair cut short and brushed back straight from the forehead. She wore a vest over a striped blouse, tight faded blue jeans, and embossed cowboy boots.

We talked first about her work.

"Sorry about not being there," she said. "I had some trouble at work. At the nine o'clock show last night my projectionist left out an entire reel of *Kagemusha*."

"Some have never wished it longer."

"Maybe so. Still, I had to fire him. You and Courty get along?"

"She was great. Talked mostly about her father."

"Oh, *him*. What did she say?"

"Basically, that he's not the worst guy in the world. She said he really enjoys the white tuxedo and playing Señor Rick at the restaurant."

"Well," Ann said, "he can have the stage. I stay back in the kitchen."

"Business OK?"

"Some nights I devein five pounds of shrimp, some nights I wait for two deuces."

Her oysters had arrived. I can still see them folded into a pale, creamy sauce with bits of caviar. We ordered a bottle of white wine.

"And you're also working at the theater?"

"Not a lot these days. I've pretty much abandoned the place for a while."

"What are you showing?"

"*Gregory's Girl*. They stayed away in droves."

"What's a bad night?"

"A hundred dollars. That would be about thirty people—total—for both shows."

"Is it any good—the movie?"

"I like it," she said. "It's set in Glasgow. Gregory is tall, gangly, covets a blonde goddess but ends up with a dark friend. He has no idea of how to pursue a woman. The one he ends up with—the girl under the tree—turns out to be the one he wanted. He lands on his feet but not by jumping off the right building. It's about feckless courtship. He reminds me a little of Ian."

"I missed him tonight."

"Well, he's fourteen. No sense of his body space. He's a cross-country runner who collides with parked cars. Had trouble learning to ride a bike. So did Chief, come to think of it."

The dessert menu came, and we agreed to share an order of pears in caramel sauce.

"I saw you on campus last week," I said, "over by Newcomb Hall. I think it was Friday."

"In the morning? I was either dropping off my ad slicks or on my way to my jazz show. I do a nine o'clock show on TJU."

"So you've got one tomorrow. What will you play?"

"Some Bill Evans—lots of piano people."

"I noticed that baby grand. It pretty well fills up the living room."

"I know. I should play it more. It's my one heirloom; it was my mother's. I played through most of college, did a junior recital. My roommate called my parents to make sure they'd send flowers. Then I went to Europe, got fat, dumped my boyfriend, and blew off my senior recital. I was very—'self-destructive.'" She raised her index fingers and wiggled them in the air to put quotation marks around the word.

The pears came, and we ordered two brandies.

Then we talked about my work.

"Are you liking your new job?" Ann asked. The question made me realize that she knew a good deal about me. We had been talking freely, having a good time, but we hadn't struck the spark. The moment was about to come.

"It's OK—a little claustrophobic. After teaching for seven years, I'm not used to regular hours or sitting all day at a desk. And it's strange to have the evenings free."

"But they're not really free, are they? Aren't you working on something?"

"On the end of something. I've almost finished a book about landscape and California. I just found a great quote by Joan Didion to use as an epigraph—about locating lessons in scenery."

"I love her stuff," Ann answered. "The novels aren't as good as the essays, though."

"No—too much riding around in cars. *Slouching towards Bethlehem* is really what got me started on my book. That first piece—I think it's called 'Some Dreamers'—is about a murder that took place on my sixteenth birthday, about five miles from where I grew up."

"The one about the woman who burns her husband in the car."

"The Volkswagen. They were going out to get a quart of milk."

Ann popped a bit of pear into her mouth. "She really does get the way people become trapped in their lives—and then want any way out. My favorite part of that book is the essay on self-respect. She has a great line about people who play around. Something about not apologizing, or looking to be let off the hook."

"I know it," I said. "That's where she talks about knowing the cost of things. People with self-respect know the cost of things."

"Right. That's the one."

That was the first night.

A few days later, I called Ann and asked her out; we began living together a few months after that. "By the way," she said, when she saw me again, "it's price, not cost, in the Didion piece. I reread it. People with self-respect know the *price* of things."

After breakfast this morning Ann leaves to watch *Imitation of Life,* and I call Luke. It turns out he got caught up in Halloween gatherings and decided to stay in town.

"But Dude, something really bad happened at work. This guy named A. had vanished. He'd asked me to cover his shift. I was over at Pete's, and some guy came in who mentioned a friend who had killed himself—and it was A. He had been in and out of school at the Corcoran; he thought he'd made a mistake, was confused about where he was headed. We had a couple of discussions, good talks. He couldn't deal with the responsibility and wanted to bail out—fall back on his parents—but didn't have a place to bail out to. He was afraid of ending up on the street. So he was rooming with the manager at Sparky's, who needed a rent partner. They had just moved into a new place, and he hadn't even unpacked his boxes. He even had a sweet girlfriend who helped him out. I talked to him a fair amount and told him about things that had happened to me—wanting to bail and then realizing that it was something you couldn't keep doing forever."

Tonight, Luke says, some friends are coming over to his place to carve pumpkins.

I'm cleaning up the living room when John Auchard calls. "I had invited Senator Edwards and his wife Elizabeth over for dinner last night, but then he got scheduled for *Meet the Press* and needed a briefing—about airport security, I think, something about Dick Armey." Elizabeth Edwards had been in John's Henry James seminar in graduate school in Chapel Hill, and at the end of the semester Lewis Leary had thrown a costume party and the class had had to come as characters from the novels. So he had made Elizabeth and John assign the characters. "She was Kate Croy from *The Wings of the Dove,* and I was Prince Amerigo from *The Golden Bowl.* I parted my hair down the middle—I had more manageable hair back then—and I had a cane, a monocle, the whole business."

"I hate it," he goes on, "when people say they're against terrorism, *but.* When the 'but' comes too soon in the sentence, I get pissed off. As if we've somehow called this down on ourselves. It's like rape: no matter what a woman's wearing, there's no excuse."

"I know what you mean," I answer. "The past two Sundays I've gotten in arguments during dinner with good friends for being so hawklike."

"It's always easy to have doubts," John says. "People want to show that they're scrupulous. But this demands action. And if this action fails, well, then, I really believe the world is in trouble."

"I get tired of tepid liberal hesitation," I say. "As a country we've done more good than harm in the world. We're all children of immigrants who came here from some wretchedness. And, unlike most other big powers, we're self-limiting."

"I think I finally realized last week," John answers, "what original sin is. It's the fact that there are moments in human life when everything you do is wrong—and yet you still have to choose to *do*."

"Yup. Hegel says that what makes for tragedy is two conflicting goods. Or conflicting bads, I suppose. Either way, you have to choose."

I have let John into my life in a particular way: of all my close friends, he is the one with whom I feel most comfortable playing at a kind of intellectual war. This is not a fight with each other but rather an effort to be equal to all that we have read and thought and to reprocess it as wit. We are both scholarship boys, proud of it, and therefore willing to show off, for each other, what we have learned. Being with John involves an uninterrupted flurry of quotes, stories, free associations, and deep thoughts. Some days, John admits, with a smile at the audacity of the comparison, he feels a little about meeting me the way Johnson did about seeing Burke on a day when he felt ill. "That fellow calls forth all my powers. Were I to see Burke now, it would kill me."

Dinner tonight with new friends. Ann makes pizzochere: potato gnocchi with cabbage, chard, fontina, and parmigiano. They are both therapists, and they are angry. "Why can't they find them and kill them?" This is the evening's refrain.

Michael mentions a navy psychiatrist who maintains that with people who have been traumatized in combat, the trick is to get them back in uniform as soon as possible. This gives them a sense of agency; it makes them feel part of a group. "But what is there for us to do?" he asks.

"Lead our lives," I answer.

At the Virginia Opera, which they recently attended, the conductor raised his baton and the orchestra burst into "The Star-Spangled Banner." "Everyone stood up and sang hard," Leslie says. "I mean everybody who goes to an opera wants to sing. Then they played the most beautiful *Tosca*. It's a music that knows that death is the mother of beauty. And I thought this is the West; this is what we are fighting for."

◊

Workers cleaning up at ground zero are dealing with soot that rose eighty stories and then fell, everywhere. They are paid $6.50 an hour and come home at night with sore throats and watery eyes. "The windows and desks are so grimy," one laborer says, "there are two inches of soot. We run these large industrial vacuum cleaners and an air purifier."

When the power company comes in with a small backhoe this morning to dig a trench for the new service, it manages to cut the roots of a maple tree. "I called the site supervisor and yelled at him," Ann says. "This whole thing is taking way too long, and today there was no one around to supervise."

I'm reading a book called *Holy Land*. It's a memoir by a man who has spent all of his almost fifty years in Lakewood, California. D. J. Waldie. When it was built, in the late 1940s, Lakewood was the largest subdivision in the world, a perfect grid of streets at right angles constructed to house workers at Douglas Aircraft. In less than three years, 17,500 homes went up. My Uncle Bill—Dad's brother—has lived in Lakewood for four decades; he lives on one of the town's few curving streets, along the golf course.

I also grew up in a California suburb, where the houses shared the same floor plan, which was rotated on the lot to create some variety. You fight hard to escape a place like that, with its strange offer of a proximity without intimacy. "Such is the attraction of suburbs," Waldie writes. "You look out your kitchen window to the bedroom window of your neighbor precisely fifteen feet away."

Dad swings by in the afternoon. He's surprised to hear that a coworker at the theater has provoked an incident with a visiting filmmaker, one of the festival honchos. It's happened before, although never when Ann was in such a house-clearing mood. "Well, he *can* go after people," Dad says. "And then he doesn't stop. Follows them the entire length of the lobby. When that happens, I just retreat into my space."

"Richard was like that," Dad continues. "He couldn't enjoy the big moment." Richard is the man who worked for Dad at James Wyatt Interiors before Mom's death and whom Dad then moved into the house and lived with for seventeen years.

Richard was my age and looked like me.

"We would work and work on a job—all the time he'd be intending to design rooms he never designed— and then the installation day would come, and he'd fall apart. One day at the swap meet, we were taking down the tent, and he left me holding close to a hundred pounds of awning—just disappeared. Why did I have to put myself through that?"

After yoga, Ann and I share a veal chop. "Do you

ever have days," she asks, "when nothing hurts?" She's had serious foot pain—a broken ankle on one leg and a dislocated toe on the other. "No," I answer, "not lately."

"Only my hand hurts," she says. "It's the real casualty of cooking in the restaurant."

After dinner, Ann says, "If I can't go to Afghanistan and help with their food shortage, I figure I'll feed people here. I'll make them eat vegetables. I mean, I don't know what starvation would be like. Even when we were poor, we had veal. So Afghanistan must be without many gleaning possibilities. And, you know, bombing doesn't really go with agriculture." The cat walks by. "We have pets—we have all these things they don't have."

◇

Charlottesville, Virginia
October 30, 2001

October 30. This is the anniversary of the day on which my mother was killed.

She died in a car accident at the age of forty-seven. The driver of the car was a woman named Celene, the leader of what we called the Group, a small collection of believers my parents had moved to San Bernardino to join in 1957.

For fourteen years, until that fall in 1971, the Group—its membership never rose above thirty—was the center of our family life. We attended gym class on Mondays and art class on Tuesdays. Every fourth Sunday, Celene held a communion ceremony. Our catechism fused elements of an animistic mysticism—we believed in reincarnation, auras, and guardian angels—with a Catholic sacrament and the Golden Rule. I participated dutifully in these rituals and began to move away from them only after leaving home.

On the day of the crash, Mom and Celene were returning from one of their frequent shopping trips to Pasadena. Celene was driving her Rambler station wagon. They had been driving east, on the straight roads that run along the base of the foothills and through abandoned wineries. They had come to a stop sign. As Celene pulled out, they were hit on the driver's side by an oncoming car.

The accident occurred near a town called Alta Loma. During the week of the funeral, Dad and I drove out to see the spot. We parked on a shoulder near the intersection and got out to look around. It was a sandy place, with no houses in view, a country of dry streambeds and an occasional windbreak of trees.

The two roads lay straight in both directions. Rows of eucalyptus ran up toward the mountains, and the road climbed with them. In that valley, the horizon puts you at the bottom of a bowl. A car coming down the road from the north would have the wind at its back, and the right of way. He hadn't had a chance to stop. And there was the stop sign, where Mom and Celene had eased out, the setting sun behind them, twenty miles from home.

It wasn't exactly belief that had put my mother in that car. She had long functioned as Celene's companion, but, by the time of the accident, her role had shifted from disciple to caretaker. For more than a decade, my mother had acted as Celene's chauffeur. Then Celene learned how to drive. But Mom still went along, as company I suppose, or out of a sense of charity for a woman whose life was dissolving around her: the Group was losing members, Celene's husband had disappeared one day, a few years earlier, while going out for a quart of milk, and the ex-con she had recently begun dating and from whom she had then tried to separate had more than once broken into her house and roughed her up.

My mother was so loyal in her commitments and so reluctant to abandon them that they held her in place long after the object of her faith had disintegrated. If hers was a formal commitment, it was also a human one. However she felt and understood the bond of fifteen years, it put her in that car, kept her available for the shopping trips to Pasadena on which only Celene did the buying, kept her riding on the passenger side.

The *Post* reports this morning that one of its employees walked into a print shop in Mexico City and was taken to a room covered with Disney cartoon posters. A man turned one of the posters around, revealing a hole containing a bag full of Mexican passports. He offered to add a phony name and photo for $150. Last year, border inspectors at San Ysidro, the link between San Diego and Tijuana, stopped fifty-two thousand people for document fraud. Mexican nationals crossing the border are now required to show a laser ID. In April, six thousand of these IDs proved to have been stolen.

During Dad's last working years in California, he employed two men who had recently arrived from Mexico. They worked hard and never missed a day. The men cut out flower shapes on a band saw and frosted them in the sandblaster. Dad airbrushed on color and arranged the flowers into bouquets. One day, José asked if he could do an arrangement. "He was so good at it that I turned the work over to him."

Dad lived underground; he didn't have a credit card or a personal checking account. Buyers at the swap meet paid in cash. Through hard work and the loyalty of his men, he was able to support himself well into his seventies. Once a year, his "illegals," as he called them, would sneak back across the border to visit their families and to leave behind the dollars they had saved.

I write two sets of Ph.D. oral exam questions for students doing dissertations with me and fax them to Maryland. Then I spend the afternoon making a huge batch of lamb sausage.

On a walk on the downtown mall, I buy a copy of

Palace Walk for Bob Schultz, who is looking for a good book out of the Middle East. It's by Naguib Mahfouz. He sets it in an upper-middle-class household in Cairo. The man of the house goes out every night to secret little taverns for wine and dancing girls. Then he returns to his wonderfully embowered home, built around a garden courtyard, where he rules the roost and his wife rubs his back. Women do not leave the house; they peer out of windows. The crisis comes when the faithful wife sneaks out to a mosque and is hit by a car. The husband is more upset because she has wandered than because she has been hurt.

Like any novel worth its salt, *Palace Walk* made me feel a strong and sustained emotion—anger at the human costs of the lived double standard. Yet it's also a wonderfully thick and in many ways appealing portrait of a Muslim world, of a city in which people are perfectly at home, and human in all of the ways we recognize. It's the first book in a trilogy. Soon after Mahfouz won the Nobel Prize, he was stabbed in the neck by an Islamic radical.

In a conversation with Ann, late this afternoon, suicide comes up. She remembers something our grill cook had said when he was found in his demolished car. They eventually got him out and set the broken bones. A zipper of stitches runs from his groin to his throat. "Just leave me here," Howard had said to the rescue squad.

"I would never say that," Ann says. "I really believe

that life has something for me. The box tops were right: there is a prize inside."

"Lately," I respond, "when I look at people, I see the inner kid. I mean, who is a grown-up? It's a good thing, in some cases. With you, for instance, there's still all that awe and energy of a girl. Lots of other people just seem undeveloped. Scared, or turning away from things. And here I am at fifty-three, a father—taking care of my father—owner of a business, a full professor, and I'm still full of all the yearnings I had when I was seventeen."

"I do feel," Ann says, "that I've been given a second chance with this restaurant. Scott came back the other night and said, 'Two young people looked at the menu and walked away.' But I don't care any longer about initiating the unappreciative. I just want to make honest food."

"I saw the guy who owns the used bookstore today," I tell her, "and he asked, 'How's the restaurant business? Have you been to the new place—Fleurie?'

"'No,' I said, 'but it's run by the guy who used to cook for us. He's French-trained; he wasn't really comfortable in an Italian situation.'

"'Well, I don't know—twenty-nine-dollar entrees in Charlottesville?'

"It's a funny town. It may work. People here either want economy or conspicuous consumption. They are not particularly interested in cooking that tries to stand firm in the middle."

225

Later on, at dinner, Ann asks, "Do you worry about him a lot?" She's asking about Luke.

"No."

"But you still have this thing in your chest."

"That's just me. That's where I put my pain."

◇

Halloween. Lots of rumors swirling around this date. It's the first full moon on the holiday in forty-six years; Giuliani masks are selling well.

Michael Jordan lost in his comeback debut last night by two points.

New York City is expected to lose one hundred thousand jobs by the end of the year. Thirty downtown restaurants are closed; business is off 40 percent for the city's eleven thousand limousine drivers. A bartender who worked in the shadow of the Trade Center poured drinks there for twenty years. The bar is gone. He stands in a line at an employment fair. "We're working people," he says. "We *work*. Without it, we're the living dead."

I spend the afternoon painting windows and listening to Springsteen's *Tracks,* songs previously recorded but never released. It's the collection he sent me, a few years back, after reading my *Five Fires,* which ends with an account of a concert on his "The Ghost of Tom

226

Joad" tour. I'm at the end of the first CD when a song comes on. "I Can't Talk Now, I'm Not Alone."

Maybe I like him because he, too, is fond of an elegiac lilt.

The chorus sounds familiar. Then I remember: it's a song Libby played for me, during the separation before our divorce. "Hearts of Stone," by Southside Johnny and the Asbury Jukes. Now it makes sense: Springsteen wrote the song, gave it to the Jukes, and they covered it and made it a hit.

> I can't talk now, I'm not alone
> So put your ear close to the phone
> 'Cause this is the last chance
> This is the last dance for hearts of stone.

It's so true to the way we harden ourselves and move on, I could almost weep.

Another sudden loss—at least that's the way it felt at the time. Libby came downstairs one night and announced that the marriage was over. Of course it took two more years before we achieved a permanent physical separation, and even after that there were second thoughts. But on the night she told me she wanted a divorce, the words seemed to come from out of the blue. And that, too, was the trouble—my complete unreadiness in the face of a demand that should have come as anything but news.

"Sudden," the book explains, "as, a *sudden* shower, death, emergency, turn for the better, or attack of the enemy."

227

Ann calls me at 7:30. "It's *slooow* here," she says. "Why don't you come over and I'll cook you dinner."

◇

Charlottesville, Virginia
November 1, 2001

"Last night was the deadest night in a long time," Ann says in bed this morning. We did twelve dinners.

"People were afraid."

"That's really too bad. Especially here. What would they do if something more—more *active* happened?"

What I fear most these says, besides the terrorists, is the return of the Secret World. For most of my conscious life I lived with a sense that vast, shadowy forces were contending over the nation's fate. The true story was the unseen one, the game of spy versus spy. For about ten years after the Berlin Wall went down, the fear went away.

Now it comes up again. Members of Sayeret Matkal, the Israeli deep-penetration unit, are rumored to have arrived in the United States a few days after September 11. This is the unit that pulled off the raid on the hijacked Air France airliner at Entebbe in 1976. Why have they come? Perhaps to aid the Pentagon's own elite undercover unit trained to slip into a country and search out nuclear weapons. The likely target: Pakistan.

Ann helps me paint a pair of windows and then takes a two-hour nap. She leaves for work at four.

Things are moving slowly on the renovation. Marvin is in a cleaning mode; yesterday he brought over his leaf blower and cleared off our street.

◇

Charlottesville, Virginia
November 2, 2001

An incident occurred at the restaurant last night. Ann is cooking; Scott and Bill are out front. It is a busy night, and around 7:30 two parties come in. One is a table of friends; the other, five women, new to L'avventura. They reject their wine, a Merlot that everybody loves. One woman orders a small salad as her dinner. As soon as their food comes out, Scott is back in the kitchen. "They say it took too long—and they don't like their scallops." Ann tells him that the food is fine. Soon he's back, with more complaints. Then he says that they're leaving. Ann takes off her apron and goes into the dining room. "Step outside, please," she says, to the table. "Why? So we won't be heard?" "Let's step outside." "They were all dressed up, Dave, but they clearly didn't get it. It turned out that they usually got together at Ruby Tuesday. So I get them outside, and I said, 'I'm sorry you did not enjoy your meal. It was as expertly cooked as all the other meals that came out at the same time. I want you to go, and never come back.'"

Military planners believe that it's going to take U.S. ground forces to defeat the Taliban—large numbers of them. The Taliban has an army of some forty-five thousand men. Now a revolt against the Taliban in southern Afghanistan brings hope. It is being led by Hamid Karzai, an ethnic Pashtun whose father was assassinated by the Taliban.

I paint three windows and then finish my new Mahfouz novel, *Madiq Alley*. Mahfouz sets the story in World War II Cairo. It reminds me of Gloria Naylor's *The Women of Brewster Place*. The alley absorbs and sustains the lives lived within it: the aging landlady who hopes at last to marry; the itinerant poet who performs nightly at the café; Zaita the cripple-maker, who turns whole men into effective beggars; Hamida, who longs to escape the alley and is seduced into prostitution; Hussein, the young man who wants to live in "the modern way" and become a "gentleman" in a home with electricity. Each character has a ruling and recognizable passion, and most of these go unrequited. That people move away and return, die or fall in love, only temporarily alters the "lakelike surface" of the alley, "and by evening whatever might have happened in the morning" is "almost forgotten."

At four I'm at my station, grating Romano for a big Friday night. We decide to open the patio one last time—the temperature reached the high seventies today—and by seven it is full. I call Dad to come in to help, and he runs bread and clears dishes until ten.

◇

Hamid Karzai, our new ally in Afghanistan, was res-
cued from capture yesterday by U.S. helicopters. The
promise of Karzai is that he represents a link with the
country's past; he's from the dominant ethnic group,
the Pashtun, who are strong around Kandahar, the center of Taliban power. Karzai has traveled often to the
United States and has lived in Pakistan since the early
1990s. While most of the Taliban is composed of the
poor and the uneducated who were then absorbed into
religious schools, Karzai represents the elites that have
been exiled or killed off. Whether a man who derives
from the traditional order can hope to govern there is
an open question.

The house is a mess—full of plaster dust and
leaves—so after Ann goes to work I vacuum and wipe
up. Then I call Luke to let him know we're driving to
New York tomorrow morning.

"Did you hear about the guy in Glen Echo?" he
asks. "He left his car unlocked, then came out in the
morning, and there was this box in the back with a
suspicious powder. Anthrax-like stuff. So he called the
cops and the FBI came and did tests, which came
out negative *and* positive. So a 'large container' was
brought in. By which they mean a huge trailer that
pulls up and then the car gets pushed into it and taken
away."

Luke has been trying to open a checking account, without any ID. "I have to bring a copy of the police report about my stolen wallet. The woman at the bank asked if I didn't have a credit card with my picture on it. And I told her 'No.' I've never had any credit cards. Unless you're locked into the credit grid, you can't get any credit. It's a Catch-22. I wonder how homeless people operate."

At six I discover that my driver's side window has been smashed. There's glass on the hood and in the front seat. Nothing has been taken; it's simple vandalism. I drive the truck to the restaurant and tell Dad, who is selling tickets next door for *Bread and Tulips,* that I need to borrow his car for the drive to New York.

After living in town for less than two years, he has become essential to our lives here.

◇

New York, New York
November 4, 2001

It's Sunday, and we're headed north. I make cornmeal pancakes while Ann packs. I haven't felt this good in weeks.

Dad comes by with a care package of bananas and cookies. "Ann, you won't believe it; they clapped after the 7:00 show last night." Dad, Luke, Ann, and I saw the movie at the beach together last summer. It was so bad—so smug and false in its happiness—that Luke

232

left halfway through to have a cigarette, a vice he rarely permits himself.

At the Holland Tunnel, there's a thirty-minute wait—for construction, not security. Traffic in the tunnel is actually light. Then we're in Manhattan, on the island. "Do you smell that?" Ann asks. It's the smell of water on ashes.

Flags in the store windows.

At the apartment, Ann makes pork chops with tomatoes and sage while Courtenay fills us in on her life.

She's just come back from an Italian-American wedding she attended with her ex-boyfriend, Steve.

"This is your mother's *first* wedding," Steve said to her. It's more than thirty years since Ann and Chief were married in the Milford Catholic Church. She wore a white mantilla, and the reception featured a fountain of asti spumante.

"You wouldn't have believed the food," Courtenay says. "For the cocktail hour, there was calamari and pickled eggplant and fried rice balls and peppers and shrimp and tomatoes and mozzarella and octopus and clams and olives. Then came dinner. Shrimp and salmon risotto and then a choice of either veal or chateaubriand. 'Please tell me they didn't put us with the lawyers,' Steve said, on the way to the table. 'Oh good, they didn't—they put us with the cops.' 'How can you tell?' I asked him. 'By the buzz cuts.' So we sat down—all the wives were about my age, wearing lots of sequins and tight things. I was in black slim-line pants. Once I said the words 'doctor' and 'Manhattan,' they pretty much stopped talking to me. You could see from their faces, and they were incredibly well preserved, that they had had harder lives. No gifts, by the way; everybody gave cash. A big pile of envelopes."

◇

New York, New York
November 5, 2001

We sleep late, and I awake with that uniquely embowered sense of being in a New York apartment. There is such a feeling of accomplishment in simply getting there that, once inside, you could happily sit tight.

There's packing the car and making a lunch for the road and heading north from a town 350 miles south. Up Virginia ridges to 66 and around the beltway to 95. Then north by northeast through Baltimore and across the Susquehanna and the Delaware. Paying the tolls. The Jersey Turnpike and its rest stops—Joyce Kilmer, Clara Barton, Vince Lombardi. Approaching the city though marshlands and utility plants. The diorama of the skyline. Then the tunnel, the sudden exit, the swoop uptown, the eruption of color and crowds and elevation and noise. The drop-off, the unloading, the cruising for a place to park. The walk back to the apartment, the nod to the doorman, the elevator up. Knock on the door—and you're in.

New York is about the distinction between the solace of a room and the fury of the street.

My first visit to the city came at the end of my first cross-country plane flight, in 1966, on the trip taking me to my freshman year at Yale. I was traveling with a high school friend who had also been admitted to the class of 1970. Somewhere over Missouri we met a junior from the college, whose name I've long since forgotten. He had a car garaged in Manhattan and offered us a ride to New Haven. We landed about an hour before dawn. The taxi lurched its way into town; I had never felt such bumpy roads before. Harlem, that was where the car was parked. In the early light, we pulled to a stop on a tenemented street. Steam poured out of manholes. Sleepy, and bewildered, I watched a woman sweep the sidewalk. She was old, and bent, and worked with a broom. The one square of pavement she cleaned over and over; the rest of the sidewalk seemed not to exist. She would sweep, and pause, and begin again, but there was no extension from the chosen space, no context for the task. The first day of the new life began with watching someone return to the yield that could be harvested from work on a small, rectangular, elected space.

Courtenay is up and out early this morning.

"She seems in good shape," Ann says. "She doesn't say things that make me worry about her inside. It's good that she's passed through the phase of having a million boyfriends."

We taxi to the hotel on Third Avenue and 24th. The Marcel. "How's business?" I ask the bellhop. "Busy. For two weeks after the tragedy—slow. But for three weeks now, very good."

It's a blustery, partly cloudy day. Perfect New York weather. On a TV in the lobby, I hear the news that the Yankees have lost the World Series.

Ann and I set out at eleven. She's due for a hair appointment at noon, so we split up and I head down Greenwich Street. There's a police checkpoint at Greenwich and Canal; only authorized vehicles are being let through. I continue walking south; the streets are empty of traffic and there's no need to stop at the lights. At Murray, the way is blocked by a green fence. A Customs officer opens the door, and I look through. A black cube of building is still standing, maybe ten stories high. A jagged piece of the Trade Center facade sticks up behind it, like a spar.

Blowing hard now, the wind is kicking up the dust. For a moment I'm blinded, staring into the sudden sun.

The ground I'm standing on has been swept clean.

Groups of people stand and look, without speaking.

I walk into St. Peter's Church, "New York's Oldest Catholic Parish." A priest is saying mass.

I walk to the east, then south again. At Fulton Street a chain-link barrier has blown over. "I think all these flags are acting like a sail," a cop says.

At Maiden Lane and Broadway a crowd is gathered.

We can see backhoes working. Sun glints off the compressed cube of metal; from this angle, the building looks flayed.

I can smell more than I can see, and the odor gets stronger as I make my way south. I'm circling the site. Suddenly this becomes my purpose.

A construction worker tells me that "If you want to get around, go half a block south and over to West." I catch another glimpse of the facade. Tall, narrow pointed Gothic arches, the way Cologne might have looked after the war. Four jets of water, hosing down the ruins.

I'm at Reston Place and South End. The wind is picking up; I can see whitecaps on the Hudson. At Battery Park City, a huge display of pink and blue teddy bears. As I head north, the Statue of Liberty and Ellis Island come into view. A tug pulls a tanker upriver.

At Vesey, I head east again. Then I'm at West and Warren Streets, where the dump trucks exiting the site are being washed down. Warren takes me back to Greenwich, and I've closed the circle.

I think about another black box, also a site of pilgrimage. In Mecca, the Kaaba stands in the center of the holy city, black and impenetrable, while Muslim pilgrims complete their journey by circling around it seven times.

But the holy is not locatable. Still, you long for a spot.

You can't always get at things by honestly describing them. Sometimes comparisons have to enter in.

Dinner with Courtenay and her doctor friend, Michelle, at the Green Monkey. "There was this cardiologist at St. Vincent's who was in D.C. when the attacks took place," Courty tells us. "He couldn't find a rental car anywhere, and he wanted to get back. So he rented a Ryder truck. He arrived at midnight, but he got there."

◇

New York, New York
November 6, 2001

Ann has had dreams last night. Bad dreams, about being pursued and trapped in a dark place. I bring coffee and a bagel back to the room while she eases up.

We walk down to an exhibit of photographs of September 11 taken by people from all over the city. It's called "A Democracy of Photographs." The room is full of 11 x 16 color xeroxes, and a crush of people. A few of the photographs get to me—a woman standing in a doorway, on the phone, her legs crossed, while a tower explodes in the distance, and a view of the towers from the ferry, with two scarved Arab heads in the foreground—but for the most part my eye lights on an image and then glides on. One frame is filled with the text of a sign that reads, "All of you taking photos I wonder if you really see whats here or if you're so concerned with getting that perfect shot. . . ." I think of Shelley saying that the deep truth is imageless. And I think of our enemy, who hails from a culture that prohibits making images of our beautiful, mortal, fallen world—and then I don't know what to think.

We take the subway up the West Side to have lunch with Miles Parker. Miles and his lover, David Van Leer, were our last visitors at the Cape; they left on September 9. We have known them since 1984, the year we spent at Princeton.

During my second year at the foundation, in Charlottesville, a friend asked me to do a stint at Princeton as a visiting lecturer in American studies, and, eager to get back into teaching, I jumped at the chance. Ann and I rented an apartment in Philadelphia, and I made the hour drive north to the campus two or three times a week. One of the first people I met there was another Americanist, David Van Leer.

David was back from a transforming year in California, where he had come out of the closet just in time to face his tenure review. He had gone to the Huntington to work on Emerson but had discovered leather bars instead. At a place called Cuffs, in Silver Lake, he had been approached by a San Diego artist with silver hair. He and Miles Parker fell in love and began the long-distance romance that would see them switching coasts, with Miles living in New York and drawing its endangered buildings while David, who did not get promoted at Princeton and who was then hired by UC Davis, pined for their apartment on 83rd Street.

Miles has been seriously ill this fall and is only recently back from the hospital. Neighbors in his apartment building found him wandering and incoherent. They got him in an ambulance, and he was kept for more than two weeks in a psych ward. "I think I lost my mind," he tells us. "I can't remember much about it." The best guess is that his HIV drugs and his painkillers interacted with alcohol and marijuana. David had to fly back from Sacramento to get him out.

"So was it a kind of amnesia?" I ask.

"I can't tell you much because I don't know it. I just wasn't there. I went there for eighteen days. I'm still so fragile, I think, 'What if I turn my head and then don't know where I am?' But on the other hand I *don't know* that I don't know where I am.

"I had lots of fantasies of religious torture and of women trying to tie me down and putting electrodes on my nipples. I must have a real thing about women.

"I swear, the hospital where I eventually ended up—I've still got burns on my wrists where they tied me down. The driver was supposed to take me to NYU Hospital but he took me to Cornell, instead. Nobody has the right to take eighteen days out of my life." His eyes look smaller; his hair is shorter and grayer.

"David couldn't get back at first, but when he did, he started the battle to rescue me. One day I'd had enough and I said to him, 'I can't be here.' According to some of the 'rule books,' I had been fighting with staff. All of my rings were stolen while I was in there. Things that I have loved. Especially my horseshoe ring, which I've owned since I was a hippie in the 1970s.

"When he got me home, I can even remember him saying, in bed, 'I'm David.' But I thought he was Marbeth, my friend next door. You can't imagine how scared I am. Nobody's calling it anything. It's modern medicine for the lower class."

We ask him how he's feeling today. "There are all these games one plays to be sane, and all of a sudden I don't know them anymore. Because of my pain, I can't do too much. I'm already thinking that I don't know how long I can tolerate this. I feel like I'm a walking crystal—I'll shatter if anything goes sideways on me. And I feel like I've ruined David's life. He was so loving when he flew back, and I feel like it's so wasted."

Ann won't hear of it. "He got to have the chance to live with the person he loved."

"Maybe. I don't know. I can't even go to the gym anymore; it's such a plastic battle."

We ask about their life after the attack. "Well, David completely lost it and went to bed for a week and a half. I wanted to watch TV. So we finally resolved it by his going out into the living room and listening to opera. He doesn't like the real world, anyway; he'd rather read it or listen to it or look at it.

"Up here, on the West Side, we crept around for

a couple of weeks. On edge and looking over our shoulders.

"The dust came up here. . . . I did three or four drawings. I expurgated it that way.

"I don't know why I went out," Miles says. He means "went crazy."

"I sure do feel things, and one of the strongest things I feel is about buildings. And I started having some literary thoughts before I went away. The one thing I thought was solid—architecture—suddenly made no sense. It turns out you can blow it over."

We look around the room, its walls covered with pen and ink drawings of historic structures on the Upper West Side, and oil paintings of flowers and friends. "For the first time in my life," Miles says, "I have more art than I have walls. Part of the joy of making art is in getting rid of it."

We walk over to Amsterdam for a pasta lunch with Miles, then say good-bye.

Dinner with Dan, Courtenay's new boyfriend, at the Mercer Kitchen. He works in financial services about two blocks south of ground zero. "As soon as the first plane hit," he says, "we started to evacuate. The air was full, it seemed, of the most beautiful confetti. After the second collision, everyone began walking or running uptown. I was on the FDR Drive with my shirt over my head. And then I saw the firefighters, headed downtown. They were young, my age or not much older. And they were going the other way, into the dust. Their faces were completely calm. 'Driving into death,' I said. It was the most heroic thing I've ever seen."

◇

Charlottesville, Virginia
November 7, 2001

"How'd you like Dan?" Courtenay asks this morning, when we say good-bye on the street.

"He's very nice," Ann answers. "Very smooth. Young, I guess. He looks a little like Steve."

She grimaces, we hug and agree to see each other at Christmas.

At home, the sheetrock is up, and the joint compound is on.

Ruth and Milton bring by the cat, who stays with them while we're away. "Bush is strangling all the terrorist monies," Ruth gloats. "They won't have enough to buy box cutters."

I call John Auchard about an upcoming oral exam. He has sent my agent his anthology of quotations from the famous about their religious beliefs. Andrew is enthusiastic but concerned about obtaining so many permissions.

"I've got this friend at Lehman Brothers who says I should approach publishers and say that royalties on the book should be paid to the World Trade Center fund. Then she suggested a final section of quotes from survivors. People in New York are telling stories beyond anything she reads in fiction."

Ann comes home discouraged; only ten people for dinner at L'avventura last night.

◇

Charlottesville, Virginia
November 8, 2001

Upstairs, Marvin is quietly mudding around the new windows. "Sheetrock man charges a hundred dollars a hole," he says. "So I get to do it, instead."

I paint a few windows and go upstairs for lunch. Marvin is chiseling out a piece of oak flooring.

"You want a hot dog?" I ask.

"No. No thanks. They're my favorite. Hot dogs and fried chicken. But I already had a potato from Wendy's."

I thank him for the wine; he's passed along a bottle from Whitehall Vineyards. "Maybe we'll have a glass later on."

"No sir. A beer, maybe. No wine for me. We went to a party after the Whitehall job. They had lots of little knickknacks to eat. And Mary said, 'Marvin, try this wine—it's so sweet.' So I took some—and, man, that stuff was sour. No sir. Just a beer for me."

"Dry, I think they call it. It's not sour, it's *dry*."

"Whatever you say—'Dan.'"

At five I drive over to see Dad's house. He's been working for weeks to get it ready for Meleesa's visit.

"So how was your trip to New York?" he asks. "Any effect on your writing?"

"No epiphanies. I feel as if the story has gone a little flat; it's hard to feel strongly in any direction during this period of . . . waiting."

"I know what you mean. There was this huge and intense event, and then we get this little Gilbert and Sullivan war. Did you hear what Rumsfeld said, about why we bomb? That the point is to kill people. It's so raw-boned."

"Pragmatic—maybe that's the best we can say. But what about you—are you feeling anxious—or excited—about Meleesa's visit?"

"Well, my life is ongoing. It's in place. This will be a very nice thing, but I'm not looking for anything to *change* it. When we talk on the phone, we mostly laugh. Like the old days."

"How long has it been—since you've seen each other?"

He thinks for a minute. "It was right before she left for New York. She came to see me. He didn't come. When was that?"

"1983. She and Larry stopped by—we met him for the first time that summer—on their way east. So it's been eighteen years."

"I don't think about it that way—in terms of how long it's been."

"The wedding was four years later, in 1987. That's the summer Barney and I drove out with the boys. And you guys were moving, to that awful apartment in Tustin, with the aqua appliances."

"That was a nadir; I was past caring about things like that. It took me years to recover from it all, the break with Meleesa. But I didn't have time to take it in then, when she asked me not to come to the wedding."

"And then Richard left, the next spring."

"Yes, he'd used everything up, so he was free to leave."

"But what was he there for, in the first place? It seems to me sort of an *All about Eve* situation. That he coveted your life."

"Well, he got it. He took all of it. Seventeen years. And he didn't even like the girls. The only way to explain it—and it's a cop-out to say so—is that it was karma. Something I had to go through."

"It was very—romantic."

"Oh yes, it was all about romance. You see, I didn't know anything about being gay. So, when he came along, well, I fell for it."

"Yes, you didn't give yourself any time to shop around."

"No, he picked me. But, you know, he was never content. Afterward, people said, 'Thank God you got rid of him.' That made it a little easier. But at the time, well . . ."

"You can be pretty stubborn in your choices."

"Do you know that in Laguna he used to go out and fuck married school teachers? They were the best he could get; he wanted young things, but they wouldn't have anything to do with him. And then he'd complain to me, that he had to 'counsel' them. By which he meant listening to their problems. That's the good thing about my time with Jake. We really cared for each other. He just couldn't make the final step. But Richard never gave me any real support. Everything was a crisis. You and Ann don't see how much you support each other—you complain about it—but you *do*."

"I know, I know, we do."

◇

Charlottesville, Virginia
November 9, 2001

"Let's roll," Bush says, in ending his speech in Atlanta last night. About thirty-two thousand Americans have taken antibiotics for anthrax. No new cases have been reported since Kathy Nguyen died in New York on October 31.

A day of resting up before cooking tonight. During prep, Sean, one of the owners of Escafé, drops by to talk about napkins. "So, I see George is working for you now."

"Yes, he breaks a lot of things," Ann says, "but he's loyal."

"He worked for us for a few days. Until, I guess, he figured out that Doug and I were lovers."

Later, at staff meal, Howard confirms the surmise. "Yeah, George told me that he worked there but that he had to leave. 'I was talking guns,' he said, 'and they were talking gay.'"

◇

Charlottesville, Virginia
November 10, 2001

The Northern Alliance has taken the city of Mazar-e-Sharif. "People are firing their guns in the air in celebration," a businessman in the city is quoted as saying. "The Taliban have run away."

The FBI is now claiming that the anthrax letters were most likely the work of a lone, angry adult male.

The devil at home. If this loner exists, he belongs to our Shadow, the part of us we have ignored, or bypassed. It's the coordination of the mailings with the attacks that makes them so horrible, since they may be *unrelated*, the fallout from an entirely different problem of hate at home. Part of the cruelty in the timing is that the mailings have divided our attention and created a kind of self-regarding dread.

Bob Schultz calls. "It's been start in the morning and fall into bed at night. Now I have to visit the classrooms of all of my colleagues. They're eleven of us, counting me."

He mentions a reading scheduled at Luther on Thursday, from his novel-in-progress about a wife who dies in a plane crash, and worries about having to summarize the story. "I'm afraid it'll sound like a pot-boiler."

"I read my 'Hardball' essay last week," he goes on. "In a Dutch town nearby, called Pelle. It even has an Amsterdam-style canal—and a windmill. They treated me royally; put me up in a nice hotel. There were people standing in the corners of the room. Afterward, I got to meet the college president—a retired air force general—who talked about a production of *Lysistrata*. His drama person was worried that it might be too racy—the Greek women going on a sex strike to stop the Peloponnesian War, and all that—and the general said, 'Don't worry about it, I'll take the heat. We used to do the play at the Academy, and I loved it. Tell them it works just fine with people who know what war really is.'"

◇

Charlottesville, Virginia
November 11, 2001

Trisha Orr calls this morning to invite us out after the opening of her painting show on Wednesday. I can't make it because I'll be at Maryland, doing three oral exams. Then Stanley Plumly calls to say he needs to opt out of one of the exams; he will be in New York all week

249

as part of the National Book Award selection committee. Too much scheduling for a Sunday morning.

Last night I went in to help out and drifted around until we got slammed at nine. At 10:30 we all sat down to a family-style meal of grilled sea bass, sautéed spinach, and mashed potatoes. Then I got out the chocolate gelato.

The sheetrocker came by and sanded the addition walls last night. The floors are covered with a layer of fine, white dust.

Afghan opposition forces took control of five northern provinces yesterday. "The Taliban are dropping everything and running away," General Dostum said.

"Oh my God, this picture of Afghan women in 1967," Ann exclaims, reading the paper this morning. "They look just like I did." They are dressed in short skirts and flats, with bouffant hairdos. "Look at them— I had that coat. A little Chesterfield with a Peter Pan collar. In fact, one of these women looks like me."

Sunday morning and its rituals. We sleep late, tired from the week. Norma comes over and puts her paws up on the bed. Her unclipped boxer ears give her a mournful, Yoda-like expression. "Big dog, big dog," Ann says, patting and kissing her. Boris the cat, curled up next to Ann, licks the dog's head.

"Coffee—I need coffee," Ann murmurs. By 10:30 we're up, and I grind the last two scoops of beans and put in some decaf for good measure. Ann reads sections of the *Post* aloud while we finish our poached eggs. The new heating system comes on, blowing warm air across the living room. Sun streams through bare tree branches and into our new windows.

During our nap, Schuyler Schultz calls from Iowa. He is graduating from Luther next spring and wants to become a chef. I mentioned to Bob that we might need a summer sauté cook, so we talk a while. He's been cooking at the hotel downtown. We commiserate about customers, and ingredients. "Just to give you an idea of how bad it is here," Schuyler says, "we get only two orders for medium rare steak a month. And I almost cried the day the manager substituted that sixty-forty stuff for real butter."

Ann is excited by the call. "I don't mind working hard now. But the idea of having to cook all summer— that's too much."

Ruth and Milton come by for dinner tonight. She's eighty and he's eighty-eight; they are devoted readers and see every movie that moves. He was a master sergeant in a troop carrier squadron during the war; when he came back, he fell in love with Ruth and her Joan Crawford high-heeled shoes. Milton gave Ann away when we got married, in 1991. His legendary memory for poetry comes up with some lines by Kipling, during dessert, from a poem called "Advice to a Young Soldier:"

> When you're wounded and left on Afghanistan's plains
> And the women come out and cut up what remains
> Then roll to your rifle and blow out your brains
> And go to your God like a soldier.

◇

At breakfast we talk about money. "At work I owe three FICA payments," Ann says, "from the way I weaseled everything into October."

I suggest paying off the credit card. "But if we do, we'll just charge it up again. And this was only a four-thousand-dollar week at the restaurant. So we're short there. I'm thinking of taking the five thousand dollars that's still sitting in my theater account since *Crouching Tiger* and paying for the new carpet.

"In order to finish the project—especially to redo the old bathroom—I'll have to borrow against my life insurance. I realize that all we've done with our lives is to buy one house and then to keep borrowing and expanding on that." At present we own the house on Rothery Road, the apartment in Washington, Ann's beach cottage, Dad's house across town, the theater, and the restaurant.

"If I select a sweater for my birthday," Ann asks, "will you buy it for me?"

I'm caulking molding when Ann calls. "Another plane just went down. An American airlines plane in Queens, with two hundred people."

"Do we know if it's terrorists?"

"Nobody knows. I thought you'd want to know."

252

I turn on the radio; my heart is racing. It's American Flight 587, with 255 passengers aboard. Out of Kennedy, to Santo Domingo. Giuliani is saying that there's no evidence yet that the crash involves terrorists. The plane has crashed in a residential neighborhood.

No plane crash is any longer exempt from the power to arrest us all. Have we lost the sense of anything still being an accident?

"Some of it fell apart before it hit," a man on the scene says. He is standing near 129th Street and Newport Avenue, in Rockaway, Queens.

And now the news reports—it is noon E.S.T.—that the Northern Alliance is within four miles of Kabul.

Courty calls. "I just want you to know that I'm fine. But things are bad here; you can't get out of the city. They're concerned about a bomb in a tunnel. I went in to work earlier, and we're rounding this afternoon. But I'm never flying again. They're saying it was probably not terrorists."

"I am not comforted. With heightened security in place, you'd think the planes would at least be mechanically sound."

"Either way, the airlines are screwed. At least fares are going to be really low. It was funny—I got up late, nothing had happened, so I just went in. 'Have you heard?' Another crash. 'Get the fuck out.' They're saying they have a problem with birds nesting."

"So now it's killer birds."

At five I call Ann. "Let's skip yoga. I'm making good

253

progress on getting the living room back. I'm washing all the wood floors with Murphy's Oil Soap."

"And you want me to come home and help you finish?"

"Yup."

"OK. I'll bring some sea bass."

In an interview, bin Laden says that "Bush is a person who loves life. And I am a person who loves death. And that is the difference Americans will never understand."

We spend the evening sorting through old LPs: copies of Buffalo Springfield, Judy Collins, the Byrds, the Yardbirds.

Around nine I call Howard. He's going to New York tomorrow, so I'll miss him at school. He's planned lots of publishing stuff, then a trip north for a reading at Colgate.

"It's part of the endless pay-for-private-school tour. I'm going to ground zero on Wednesday morning. All of the reasons why one would hesitate are the reasons to do it."

About the crash today, he says this: "You know what's awful? When you're relieved that something actually *was* an accident. It's the oscillation between two terrible options. Jane just made comfort food—chicken stew. Emma cuts to the chase: 'I hope you're not flying, Dad.' 'No, I'm taking the train.'"

◇

Double headlines this morning: "At Least 260 Dead as Jet Plunges into N.Y." And: "Taliban Flees Afghan Capital."

We are winning this war.

Mazur-e-Sharif. Taloqan. Herat. And now Kabul. Except for Kunduz, the Northern Alliance controls the north.

Results from Florida are finally in. In a selective recount, Bush wins. In a statewide recount of all ballots, Gore wins, by perhaps as few as sixty votes.

Yesterday's crash was an accident. Yet investigators say, "We're utterly baffled." Both engines appear to have fallen away, an extraordinary event.

It's been a fall of burning and divided attention. One catastrophe eclipses another, each moving us a little further away from the real terror.

Ismail Khan, who has conquered Herat, once sponsored parades in the city that featured Special Forces teams that parachuted into the celebrations and skinned live snakes with their teeth.

Dad calls. "Do you think this crash will affect Meleesa's plans?" He's at the restaurant, putting up Christmas decorations. He has dyed tulle in tea to create a kind of off-copper color. "If it's easy, it's good," he says. "It all went up so fast."

Ann calls a little later. "It looks lovely," she says.

"Like my tiled shower, it looks better than I imagined it would."

After a dinner of smoked salmon, Ann walks to a piano-violin concert on campus. I call Dad and ask him to come over. "I need help picking out paint colors."

"Today, putting up those garlands over the windows, I had that guilty feeling," he tells me, over a cup of tea. "Like I used to have when I was making something. The sense that this is too easy."

"But isn't the only kind of work worth having," I respond, "in some way a kind of play? Otherwise, it's all just—labor."

"Yes. That's right. Any sort of consequence worth having depends upon being free to let things happen. In my family, you know, after Dad lost the bank, in the early 1930s, we had this false macho thing about work. That it had to hurt. And my father hated work. But he couldn't get out from under it—the raising the chickens, the worms, the dogs. That's why I was so amazed when I got to go to Art Center—you mean there's something beyond picking worms?"

We talk a little about my sister's visit, now only a week away.

"Well, as far as Meleesa's concerned, I'm in better shape than she's ever seen me. I came here to die. And I've never felt better in my life."

"You're . . . unencumbered."

"Yes, there's no one trying to steal my energy."

"No appendages. You're all smoothed off."

Washington, D.C.
November 14, 2001

Is it possible to assert a day of good news? Bush and Putin have announced major nuclear arms cuts that will reduce arsenals by two-thirds.

And the Northern Alliance has moved into Kabul. The Taliban leader Omar admonishes his retreating troops not to go "hither and thither . . . like a slaughtered chicken that falls and dies."

The black box of the plane that crashed in Queens on Monday records the struggle of the pilot to maintain control as the tail fell off.

At nine I head north to Maryland, where I'm scheduled for three Ph.D. oral exams in three days. These are invariably disappointing, since the candidate cannot possibly give back in answers what he brings to the table in anxiety. Our first candidate does fine; his subject is "Life Writing," the new name for autobiography.

"Meet me at the Mocha Hut," John Auchard says, when I pick up my office phone. "Up Arkansas to 14th." It's a fully barred storefront in a neighborhood of thrift shops and bodegas. I'm starving and exhausted— it must be switching worlds—so I order a bowl of lentil soup and chai tea.

"Recently I've been reaching out to more people in the department," John says. "I had Brian and Sangeeta over, and it was good. It turns out that he's a funda-mentalist atheist. He has it all logically worked out."

"It's not something it pays to be too sure about." Although I think, as I say this, that the description has sometimes applied to me. "Isn't it finally a matter of personal experience? Whether or not one feels God as being there? In my case, it seems important to believe that I'm going to die in order for all this to mean something. That it's my one and only chance. But being able to live like that depends, in part, on having been lucky—on having had a good life."

"Well," John says, "I keep inviting people over. What's interesting is how few seem really there. You know the saying, 'The pot's warm. But there ain't gonna be no tea.'"

"I know it."

I'm back at the apartment napping when Luke comes in, around six. The place is filling up with paintings. He's like Miles, except that in his case, he has more art than he has *floor*.

We walk over to the Calvert Café. Luke orders chicken with pine nuts and onions and devours it. I have a lamb kebab. He's finished *The Lord of the Rings*.

"The best part is when they get back to the Shire. Tolkien is much better on the hobbits—he has more feeling for them—than on the human characters. It's sort of a housekeeping situation; things keep happening at home while the quest has been going on. The bad wizard Saruman is still around, trying to stir things up. He sort of presents himself to Frodo—tempts him to take revenge—but Frodo won't do it. The evil forces have been overcome; it's like all the power has been equalized, but energy has also been drained away. Everyone is a little diminished. So, it's time to leave."

"To the Gray Havens. It's kind of like sailing to North America."

"Well, the West is where they came from. Middle Earth is a place they colonized. So it's like going home."

By eight I'm in bed. Luke makes a few phone calls and then goes out.

Going home. The phrase echoes in my mind. The most painful thing in my life—even sharper than losing my mother when I was twenty-three, although that loss has proven more unmendable—was the separation from Luke. Libby moved him back to New Jersey when he was four. I worked hard to get to him over the years, driving north when I could, having him down for largely abortive visits to Charlottesville. Luke had set himself against my choice of Ann and the new family, and they were not particularly interested in blending him in. It quickly became clear that I was going to have to compartmentalize my loves.

There's a letter from me to Bob Schultz that records the Thanksgiving of 1988. I remember sitting on our back porch, alone, while the house was full of noise, thinking in despair that Luke was only a mile across town—his mother had brought him down for the holiday to visit old friends. We had one day together, the day after Thanksgiving:

The kids came home—all three of them. It was supposed to be a good time. Luke was only here on Friday and I taught him how to chop wood. Ian and Courtenay just left, after five days home. Ann was nervous before hand but got into the visit as it went along. The high point was Friday evening. Luke and I came back to the house after seeing *Babette's Feast* at Vinegar Hill. There was a dinner party in progress; some friends, some strangers. Lights, food, noise. We burst in and Courtenay yelled, "Dave—Meleesa's had a baby!" (My second sister.) Dogs are barking, people yelling. I go downstairs to the phone. A nine-pound six-ounce girl, Katherine. Everybody's fine.

It's a haunted week, and the ghosts came back to me this year.

Ann worries that we spend all our time recovering from the bad times, making up. I tell her that's the way it is with people. But I really don't know. Not much happiness out there, when I look around. A lot of patience, putting-up-with. Good rhythms that break down. I can live with it if I'm not always stretched toward the big questions, the Should We End It All Talk.

Then I lose heart and figure better sooner than later. But actually I've been the one to defend the idea of a future, something taken on faith. We've switched roles on that one. Used to be I was always thinking about packing my bags. Now these fantasies have become almost a way of staying, of running through the fact that, yes, I will.

When Luke was fifteen, we almost lost him. The drugs and the skipped school and the untreated depression culminated in three suicide attempts and three stays in private and county mental hospitals. His mother finally placed him in a program in the desert that took burnt-out kids and walked them across central Utah for ten, sometimes twenty miles a day. After Survival came the Expedition phase, where the group was given handcarts to pull. Once he finished the Aspen program, Luke flew to Alabama, where he spent the next fifteen months at Three Springs, living with a counselor and a dozen boys in a cabin in the woods. Up at 7:00 to cook breakfast. Walk down the hill for chores or laundry. Morning classes. Lunch at the dining hall, or KP. More school, maybe some basketball. Dinner, which the boys cooked themselves. To the campfire for nightly meeting. Lights out by nine.

Luke stuck with the program and graduated surrounded by family and friends in a sun-baked field. "It was the best thing I ever did," he said more than once. We trusted that, that and the obvious changes for the better, trusted it all enough, by the summer of 1996, to let him move back home.

By Christmas of his senior year, he had totaled his Taurus and started drinking again. He dropped out of high school two weeks before graduation; his mother threw him out of the house a few weeks after that.

The turning point came that summer, when Luke moved to Charlottesville. He found a little apartment across town, worked as a cook at Tokyo Rose, became a DJ at WTJU. Over the year, he and Ann became friends. The best thing was that they often sided together in arguments against me.

What I have come to realize, after Luke moved south again this summer and spent it with us, is that his not having grown up with me allowed him to accept and maybe even to take on many of my interests. I was not a father in the house to be resisted. I have always loved books and now have a son who reads more of them than I do. He has become a deeply responsive young man, without my burden of seriousness. Although he did inherit my depression, something he deals with by lifting weights an hour a day.

Now that Luke is so thoroughly a part of my life, it gets easier to consider the intervening years. He never made many direct complaints; he was too proud to place any strong claim on my affections. But I do remember the day on which he left town and now realize that, even then, Luke knew what it was to grieve.

It was a June day in 1983; Libby called to say that she was packed up and ready to head north to New Jersey. I drove over to Lexington Avenue to say good-bye. Her Rabbit was parked out back, under the elm tree, and, after a last tour of the house together, the house it was now my responsibility to sell, I walked Libby and Luke out to the car.

It wasn't clear if we were to make our farewells before the riders got in; there was an awkwardness, a reluctance to open doors. I picked Luke up and held him for a long minute. The baby fat was nearly gone; he was on his way to becoming a tall and bony boy. He gave me a strong hug. Then I put him down. I turned to his mother. She had started to cry. My eyes were clear. We took each other in our arms. It was a warm day, and I was wearing shorts. As we stood there, each giving the person we had known for fifteen years a last squeeze, Luke bent over and kissed me on the knee.

His touch went through me like a shot: then I knew that Luke understood it all. He had found a way to let me know that he knew, and it remains a wonder to this day that the most compassion ever shown me in my life came by way of a four-and-a-half-year-old boy.

◇

Washington, D.C.
November 15, 2001

I sleep around the clock. It must be Monday, and all that work on my knees. I washed every wood floor in the house.

In southern Afghanistan, Pashtun groups are rising against the Taliban. It now controls only the southwest corner of the country, and one city in the north. U.S. Special Forces have been helicoptered in to set up road blocks in the south, where they hope to capture fleeing members of al Qaeda and even bin Laden, who has been moving from place to place in Kandahar and neighboring provinces.

"They destroyed all the facilities here," a commander in the Northern Alliance says about the Taliban, as they fled Kabul. "They took whatever they could. Then they broke all the locks."

After coffee, Luke and I walk over to Riggs Bank and open a joint checking account for his use. He is still without ID and has been using money orders to pay his bills.

An oral exam this afternoon for a student of John Auchard. A few minutes beforehand, he comes into my office.

"I have this lovely student who asks the most wonderful questions—like, 'Do you think that James was fragile?' 'No,' I told her, 'no one who writes fifty volumes could be.'"

"He was one of the toughest people who ever lived. What he was was discreet."

"She complained about him a little. She said that she read him and read him, but the characters still seemed remote. 'Well,' I told her, 'that's how people are.'"

"Ah, people. People are remote even from themselves."

Later on, John and I meet at his apartment. I've bought sausage, and spinach, and bread—and a bottle of wine—to make dinner, but he claims that his house is a mess and that we must eat out. Before we do, he pours us each a glass of sherry.

"Was that strange for you today," I ask him, "when I asked you to fix my cow lick?" Luke does not have a comb or a brush at the apartment, and after I worked in the gel this morning I had no way to finish the job.

"No—I actually liked it. It made me realize for the first time that you were physically vain. And you didn't look so—smooth. I deal with cowlicks all the time. You know Jeannie; she has quite a wit. Well, the other day, she walked by me and said, 'Ah, *genius* hair.'"

As it does so often, our conversation turns to travel. John tells a story I've heard before, one I'm happy to hear again.

"I was in New York, on my way to France. And I was feeling very bad, probably clinically depressed. I was walking past St. Patrick's, and I went in. I said to the attendant that I'd like to see a priest. 'And make it a good priest.' She paused, nodded, and disappeared.

"I sat in a little chapel off to the side, and pretty soon the priest showed up. He was young, Spanish. So I began to talk. 'I'm traveling to France,' I told him, 'and I'm worried about being alone.' Of course I travel alone all the time, and love it, but on this occasion I couldn't face it."

"Then the priest said something—he had a thick accent—and this is what I heard. 'The Lord meant for us all to live in Paris.'"

"Well, I thought, this is a pretty worldly priest. I mean, if you can swing it, there's no quarreling with that. So I said something in reply, about the logistics of doing that."

"He seemed a little confused, and then he smiled. 'You seem to have misunderstood. What I said, what I meant to say, is 'The Lord meant for us all to live in *pairs*.'"

Good advice, we agree, either way.

John, my father, and my son all live alone, and yet each in his own way looks to me complete. John has said about himself, more than once, "I don't have a center to my life." It's a way of acknowledging that he and I live differently and that marriage can provide an anchor or a focus that living alone does not. John's tone, when he says this, is of someone giving a description rather than making a complaint. He has solved the problem of attachment by bringing to his travels and his friendships and to the warmly lit space of his apartment, where he has prepared for me so many expert meals, an attention that is scrupulous and self-delighting.

After dinner with John at Fio's I walk back to my apartment and find Luke ready for bed. He sleeps in the bedroom, and I use the queen-sized futon in the living room. It's not a large apartment, the doors are open, and so we fall into an old habit, one that developed over years of sharing motel rooms together, all over the East Coast, on those weekends when I would drive north or he would fly south, the habit of talking late into the night, about our feelings and our lives. Tonight we speculate on how long it will take to capture

Osama bin Laden. "Yeah, I read that too," he says, about some claim I've lifted from the *Post*. He's quick, these days, to catch me in these borrowings. The conversation trails off, we're quiet for a while, and then Luke begins again, another topic, another meander through the dark.

◇

Charlottesville, Virginia
November 16, 2001

At the third oral exam, held this morning, I meet three new young colleagues, all just arrived this fall. Two of them are Berkeley graduates. I mention that I got my degree there as well. "I was there from '70 to '75."

"You got your Ph.D. in five years?"

"Yes. I had Stanley Fish breathing down my neck. It was a great time to be there."

"Where did you live?'

"Jackson and Solano, in Albany. We had a little duplex that rented for $150 a month. I had a lovely garden."

More than my class work, more than my dissertation, even more than my first marriage, which I mostly enjoyed, during those five years, what I remember from that time is that garden.

Spring comes early in the East Bay; by mid–February the plum trees are in bloom. I grew orange and yellow calendulas during the winter months and pulled them up in early March. Then I began planting vegetables and flowers in alternating rows. Beans, carrots, and lettuce, a row of phlox and marigolds, then mounds for pumpkins and cucumbers. In the far corner of the lot, at one end of the annual garden, there was a prolific fig tree. I had two rows of strawberries along the garden path, summer bloomers in that climate. During a good summer without rain I could pick a cup or two of berries a day. The annuals ran straight toward the fence and into a five-foot stand of red geraniums that grew like weeds. I had a little rectangle of lawn bordered with eight rose bushes; by June there were two-foot stems on the blood-red Lincoln rose. California poppies came up everywhere, and I let them go. Against the other fence I staked up sweet peas in the shadow of my huge camellia bushes. Right in the middle of things, about five feet high, grew a Meyer lemon tree. I filled bowls with fruit so sweet we didn't need to add sugar to our lemonade.

I discovered the garden soon after my mother died and, in good weather, spent hours there.

I'm back in Charlottesville by three o'clock and give Meleesa a call. She's in the middle of directing rehearsals for her Neil Simon–Chekhov adaptation.

"It's the only way I'd get close to Neil Simon," she says. "But doing all the interesting Chekhov adaptations by different authors would have killed us on royalties. I tell you—I need a break; I've been working steadily for two and a half years."

"Are you anxious about next week?"

"Not really. Just nervous. I'm really glad we're coming. It's going to be a big deal."

"Dad's been dealing with it by decorating his house. He's got three different colors in the big room—butterscotch and a light yellow and a light blue. He even recolored the background of one of his big flower paintings to blend it into the decor. He's been buying antiques and refinishing them; it's as if he's finally moving in, after being there for more than a year."

"Well, it's Dad and Larry that I'm most worried about." They have never met and have had a few violent encounters over the phone.

"In some sense it's a side story," I answer. " In-law relationships are usually vexed."

"I just want everybody to give everybody a chance. And I expect that everybody will."

"My sense is that it will be so unreal that it will be doable."

"Well, it's time, and it needs to happen. I expect that everybody will be very busy charming everybody else."

"And we have the two birthdays to worry about. 'Twenty-three on the twenty-third'; that's how Luke has been referring to himself."

"Yes, and my little bean is going to be thirteen on Sunday."

"She sounds thirteen going on thirty-five. When I called last night and talked to her, she was utterly composed. I think she may have used the word 'projected,' about an expectation or a plan for this weekend."

"Yeah, she's very grown-up, but I can still make her giggle."

◇

Charlottesville, Virginia
November 17, 2001

Just when the war in Afghanistan seems almost won, they have found another anthrax letter. It was mailed to Senator Leahy. Leahy and Daschle. The pattern is fairly clear; the sender looks to be one of our own, from the far right wing.

U.S. forces are now engaging the Taliban in direct combat. Reports out of Kabul claim that Muhammed Atef, bin Laden's right-hand man, was killed this week in a bombing raid. The Taliban is also reported to have abandoned Kandahar, its stronghold, and to have turned it over to Pashtun tribal chiefs. Ramadan begins today.

At nine I call Bob Schultz. He gave a public reading from his work this week at Luther. He led off with his novel in progress, a chapter in which a man goes to Seattle in search of his runaway son.

"I played it safe," Bob says. "I didn't read from the later stuff. Then I finished with the baseball piece. People love that. But there wasn't much of a turnout;

270

only about thirty people. When I used to give read-
ings, I filled the room. I've taken so many leaves that
students don't know who I am anymore. I'm forgotten,
but not gone. Students these days seem to go only to
what's required."

"I was thinking, the other day," I answer, "about
being young and in Berkeley. We were always scouting
out epiphanies. Going to see Gary Snyder, or Adrienne
Rich, or Galway Kinnell. Every week there was someone amazing in front of me."

"Here, there's this ethic of 'busyness.' They're half
asleep in class."

I ask about his Thanksgiving plans and then remind
him about Meleesa's visit.

"This will be a big one," he says. "Thanksgiving has
always been so fraught for you."

He's right about that. It's a day crowded with
anniversaries.

My parents were married on Thanksgiving day in
1944. My mother was twenty years old. That day also
happened to be her birthday. November 26.

Luke was born on Thanksgiving in 1978. November 23.

Kate, Meleesa's daughter, was born on November 25.

Ann's mother, Anita, died six years ago on November 19.

Voisine, our boxer, died during Thanksgiving dinner in 1989.

This was the time of year when Ann and I split up, for three weeks, fourteen years ago.

We didn't get back together in time for her birthday, on December 2.

I didn't know that there was a thing called an "anniversary effect" until Phil Halapin told me about it.

◇

Charlottesville, Virginia
November 18, 2001

"So what if I decide I want to keep the restaurant?" Ann says this morning.

"That's fine. It was you we were concerned about in the first place."

"But you're part of it, too."

"Sure. But I know how to protect myself, when to withdraw. It was your not having fun with it that brought this all up."

"Well, right now I'm ready to have Schuyler sign on for the summer."

"Bob said Schuyler thought it would be good to work out here. 'Sounds like they've got a big menu.' I disabused him of that. The hotel where Schuyler's been cooking also may close. It just keeps losing money; in northern Iowa, Bob says, people just can't imagine paying fifteen dollars for an entrée."

It turns out that the Taliban has not surrendered Kandahar and that it will fight for it.

272

Ann cuts my hair on the back deck in a warm November sun.

We spend the afternoon priming sheetrock and painting windows.

At five a call from Ian, whose truck has broken down in Fogelsville, Pennsylvania, on the way back from a visit to his sister in New York. I fax him a credit card number so that he can buy a room.

Baked sweet potatoes for dinner.

Afterward, we go to see *Heist*. It's a movie full of empty double-crosses. Ann has one comment to offer. "He's the sexiest man in the world," she says, about Gene Hackman.

◈

Charlottesville, Virginia
November 19, 2001

Ann is talking to Ruth on the phone about cooking a turkey. She has the assignment for Thursday. The question of stuffing comes up—how much to put in. "I'm pretty much of a crammer," Ann says.

The day is spent painting. We pick John Auchard's bedroom color—a buttery yellow—for the new room. "This is a great color," Ann says, once I get the ceiling on.

I leave Phil Halapin's office this morning with a box of Effexor and a box of Viagra. "I guess we're chemical beings," I say, sometime during the hour.

The new carpet is in today. It's a beautiful toast color. "Everything looks like the dog now," Ann says.

"Well, she's the best color there is."

Luke calls just before dinner. He's taking a bus down on Wednesday. "How old's Kate going to be?"

"Thirteen."

"Do you know what she's into?"

"Art supplies. You might also give her a little painting. But we can shop when you get down here."

"Cool. It's all good. That way I can get a sense of her."

An envelope arrives today from Miles in New York. Inside are two drawings, both pen and ink. One is printed in the *Chelsea Clinton News,* his usual venue. Beach grass in the foreground, cottages behind. The caption reads "View from Ann & David's House. Dennis. Cape Cod. Robert Miles Parker. 9.7.2001." The second drawing is dated "9.17.2001." Its caption reads "View from the Staten Island Ferry." The buildings of lower Manhattan, and behind them a billow of smoke.

The Before and the After. Straddling time.

The mindlessness of painting walls today induces thought. I end up pondering the seven deadly sins, and which of them are mine.

Anger and pride and gluttony for sure, as these pages show. Not much sloth; I work pretty hard. And very little envy. I have gone after what I wanted and been fortunate in getting it. The other two sins I forget.

Perhaps this is inevitably a self-congratulatory exercise.

Ann and I end up talking about envy. "Do you have any?" I ask.

"Not much. I do envy the young."

"I regret the loss of energy, but I don't envy the young. I wouldn't want to be young again. I wasn't that happy."

"No, you're right. The other night, I came out into the dining room, and some people were leaving, and Scott and Barbara were saying good-bye. And the man looked at me and said, 'Is that the chef?' They said, 'Yes.' And he said, 'This was great.'"

"You are a great chef."

"I don't need to be a great chef. I just want to be acknowledged as the chef. All you have to do, it turns out, is wear the costume."

At dinner, after the shrimp and spaghetti and the wine, I say to Ann, "Is exhaustion one of the seven deadly sins?"

"'What's the most formidable piece of growth in your life?' you asked me a while ago," Ann replies. "And you said that for you it was going to Yale and that for me, you thought, it was marrying Chief Gordon."

The house is still full of the books he bought. It was an odd thing to say, but I halfway believe it. "It was the first outsized thing that had happened to you, from the way you tell it."

"He had such a grand vision of what his life was going to be. My father said things to me, when I was growing up, like 'Why don't you become an interpreter at the UN?' There was a snowball's chance in hell I was going to become that. Those immigrant parents, you know, they don't provide any steps between the thought and how you get there. And there was Chief, with all those steps. We did opera and ballet and movies and books and talked constantly about them. It's interesting, though—eventually I became language phobic. Last week, when Miguel came in to wash dishes, I was anxious about speaking Spanish. And he was fine. So what's my problem with going to foreign countries?"

"I've been thinking about the nature of friendship," Howard says, when he calls later that evening. "About the sheer work it takes just to keep in touch. And that it's all for the best, of course. But having close friends is sort of like, well, a parallel career.

"New York was extremely complicated. Our therapist had asked a question of us, last week. 'What is all this stuff about phone calls back home?' My calling Jane from the office eight, ten times a day. When there was no answer, I noticed her—the therapist—getting irritable, for the first time. Then she asked another question: 'Isn't it clear that somebody's trying to make contact?'

"I walked down to ground zero at 5:30 in the morning. I don't know. Christ. I wasn't quite prepared.

There's a feeling of *souls* being there. Did you see the people applauding?"

"No."

"Well, there are groups of people at the site working in six to seven hour shifts, sifting through the remains. When they find anything—a ring, a fingernail, a knuckle—they pull it out and send it to a lab. And when some little thing is found, the people watching the work applaud. I just totally burst into tears.

"Midtown was empty for me. But then I got this invitation to read at the 12th Street Fire Station. So I canceled my dinner reservations and went down there. It was widows and orphans. No one got through the reading. At one point a group of Muslim women came in; one of them had lost a brother. And they set up this warbling chant, the most grief-stricken sound. Like wolves. They gave me a short story to read by a Somali writer. I got about two pages in and couldn't go on.— These wounds are going to be raw for many many years. Such an accumulation of sadness.

"So I called home a lot. I insisted on it. I finally said to Jane that when certain kinds of contacts aren't happening, then you need to diversify."

In listening to him, I feel the need to say something, about his willingness to keep reaching out. "You still care and want something," I say, "and that will come across."

"I don't know, David. There's warmth; we don't walk into the house and go to separate corners. Lately

277

I've been thinking that you need to go with a person's affections. You need to set out on purpose to make them happy."

◇

Charlottesville, Virginia
November 20, 2001

On the day my mother was killed, in 1971, Meleesa was fourteen. I was in my second year of graduate school at Berkeley, living with Libby in the duplex on Solano Avenue. The call came at midnight.

I got up and sat on the stairs to answer it. It was my father. "Son, I have some terrible news." He faltered. Libby had taken a seat beside me. When she saw my face, she began to cry. My father went on. "Your mother was killed today."

We caught a taxi in an hour, flew south, and arrived before sunrise. A young man named Richard, one of Dad's employees, met us at the airport and drove us home. I spent the week in my father's house, arranging the funeral, receiving the guests. I did not cry or seem to mourn. I went back to school and got my papers in on time. My teachers never knew. We went south a lot after that, to the houses along the coast my father moved in and out of as often as once a year.

What does a girl take from a mother she has known for only fourteen years?

She had her story of what happened. Dad's account

was the one I heard first and the one that took precedence in my mind; Meleesa's didn't come to me until years afterward.

Dad told us that the news had come to him at about five in the afternoon. He had been unpacking a delivery at the back of the store when the phone rang. It was Meleesa. She had come home from school and was calling to say that "the house is full of smoke." She had looked everywhere but could find no fire. At that moment, a car drove behind the store and stopped. It was a sheriff's car, and Dad walked out to meet it. The driver got out of the car and began walking toward Dad. And then, before the uniformed man had spoken or made any sign, Dad cried out to him, or to the very air itself, "What will we do with the bodies?"

Meleesa remembered the day differently:

"I spent the afternoon calling Celene's house. I wanted Mom to get home because I was planning to spend the night at a friend's house, and she was supposed to drive me there. Finally, I called the store to see if they had heard from her, and they hadn't. Dad and Richard eventually came home—Richard had been living with us for a few months—I don't know what time it was, but it was dark. We started dinner and didn't voice anything beyond 'Maybe they had car trouble.' This was of course ridiculous—the notion that Mom would not find a way to call if there was trouble was absurd.

"Anyway, finally there was a knock on the door, and I answered. A man said, 'Is this the residence of Alice

279

Joy Wyatt?' I said, 'Yes, but she's not at home.' By that time, Dad was there. He pushed me out of the way and went outside, shutting the door. At some point, Richard joined them. I watched—from the dining room window—these three men stand in a circle, heads down, talking slowly. Finally, they walked back to the house. I met them at the door, and Dad said, 'They're gone.' We sent Madeline to watch TV—it took a while to work up the courage to tell her. I don't remember if he held me or not or if I cried then. At some point, we started making calls. I sat on the floor and read him the phone numbers, and Dad called people."

At the end of the funeral week, my father drove us back to the airport. At the gate, he turned to Libby and said, about me, "Be careful with him. He needs adoration." We said our good-byes and boarded the plane. As we took off, we flew parallel to the foothills and then banked north over the high mountains.

So the new life began. Richard stayed on, Dad closed the store a year or so later, and the family began its migration toward the ocean. By the time that life ended, twenty-five years later, Dad was alone.

But during the first years after her mother died, Meleesa and her father were about as close as people can get. She was now the woman of the house—Madeline was only four when her mother died—and his heart's darling to begin with. I visited only on holidays and in the summer, but what I saw when I did go home was two people struggling to fill a huge hole and giving each other a support and love so desperate that it crossed over into a precarious adoration. It wasn't something that could last, and when it fell apart, in Meleesa's mid-twenties, it collapsed under the pressure of all that had been said and felt, and especially of all that had not been. I watched it happen from a distance, a distance I was glad to have, but I did sometimes glimpse the terrifying solitude my sister and my father shared as they tried to patch together a life when its center had been ripped away.

◇

Charlottesville, Virginia
November 21, 2001

Meleesa is due in at three today.

In bed this morning, Ann says, "That was quite a conversation last night. When I said to you, 'I know that you're devoted to me.' And you said, 'Yes, I am.' I said it without feeling any defenses. I mean, how many women approaching sixty can say that to their husbands? Uh oh—my face is getting wet."

Marvin calls at nine. "Just checkin' in. We're going to get that wood floor in today. Sanders will come in next week. And the plumbers, too, to set the fixtures in the new bathroom. And I called somebody to get that trash out front hauled away."

The latest crisis: our turkey, for a dinner at Barney's of nineteen people, weighs only nine pounds. Ann ordered it from Polyface, the organic coop in the Shenandoah Valley that supplies us with our best produce. "Art said because of the drought there was nothing for them to eat this year." It looks like a big chicken.

We call Mary, and she agrees to buy an additional bird.

I spend the afternoon waiting at the house. Dad checks in occasionally. "They must have gotten stuck in traffic." Around five a white car pulls up.

"You made it!" I say, as they unfold from the car. Kate is a tall thirteen, with long black hair. Larry has a buzz cut. Meleesa is grinning from ear to ear.

"I'm so nervous," she says. "Can I have a little drink?" I pour her some Irish whiskey and give them a tour of the building project.

"Well, I guess we should go over." We pile into my car and drive across town to Dad's house.

"Oh look—there he is," Meleesa says, when she gets out of the car. Through the windows, we can see him moving toward the front door. He opens it before we can knock.

Then they are holding each other. "This is my daughter, Kate," Meleesa says, "and this is my husband, Larry." I'm trailing behind. "This is my father."

"You look so good, Dad," she says. He is beaming. And, like Ann this morning, his face is wet. "How are you?"

"If I were any better," he says, "I'd fly away."

Then he gives them a tour of the house. "This is

your room," he says, to Meleesa and Larry. He has painted the walls pink, bought new pillows, hung a mirror over the bed. We walk down the hall. "And this is your room, Kate." A four-poster single bed, with a pink and white quilt. On the wall, he has painted an imaginary window. Over the bed he has hung a pencil drawing of the Delphic Sybil, from the ceiling of the Sistine Chapel. It is a drawing Mom did in the 1960s, a careful rendition. She was a faithful copyist. Kate admires it, and Dad says, "It was your grandmother's. I want you to take it home."

The house is full of photographs, some of people—Larry and Kate—Dad has never before met. There is one out of the *LA Times* of a woman in a sheath dress wearing a star-shaped headdress that swoops down to her toes and six feet above her head, something he built for Crosley's Florist in the 1950s. He quotes Mom on the subject. "Oh, I get it. Some men go fishing; you do headdresses."

The photograph that gets to me is of Mom and Dad. They're standing in the forest in the mountains, where we lived when I was very young. He has his arm around her neck as she leans into him. They're both in pants, with clay on their clothes from working in the pottery. Young, slim, and smiling. Two happy people in love.

Dad and I head to the restaurant and let them settle in. "Meleesa looks good," he says. "She hasn't changed a bit."

Luke calls from the house a little later. He has had a seven-hour bus ride from D.C. "Pretty hellacious," he says. "I was sitting next to this guy who looked like a Buddha and smelled like urine. And also like somebody had tried to wash him down with Comet."

We all meet at the restaurant for dinner at eight. I chat with Larry about his work. He's still a lawyer for a private firm that contracts out as public defenders. Luke talks with Kate, who tells him that she wants to be president when she grows up. Someone asks Dad what is different about life in Virginia. His reply: "People here drive over the center line."

They love the food; they love Dad's decorations; everyone acts well. Afterward, Meleesa gives me a hug and says, "Isn't it amazing?"

L'avventura means "adventure," or, as John Auchard tells us, "midlife affair." We started the restaurant, in part, as a response to the diminishing role of family in our lives—we came up with the idea in the spring after Ann's mother, Anita, died—and yet on this November night it has afforded the place where my father and my son and my sister and I sit down together for the first time in our lives.

Dad and Luke and I gather back at Rothery Road. Luke beds down in the loft, but his voice drifts down and joins our conversation. We range around, like old friends. At one point Luke recalls a *Times* article about the history of hair in Islam. "It turns out that no prophet of record has been shaved. So they got on this thing about having beards. But nowhere is it written. And, as far as women go, there's a big hang-up on the word 'ornament.' Women aren't supposed to display their 'ornaments' in the street. Whatever that means. The trouble is, they've taken it to mean everything."

Ann comes home late; it's been a big night. "How's it going?" she asks, as we climb into bed.

"Couldn't be better," I answer. "It's just like nothing at all has happened."

◇

Charlottesville, Virginia
November 22, 2001

Six weeks from today, Ann and I will find ourselves in London. It's my first trip; Ann, who has visited the city a score of times, decided that after four months we had finally earned that evening alone together.

"Remember that last day we spent in London?" she will ask, one morning after we've flown home. "We slept late, had breakfast in bed, did a little fucking, went back to sleep. God, it was so nice to have that quiet hotel. When we woke up, it was almost dark. And then we took the tube to the City, of all places. And it was even darker, and so empty. Not a person on the streets. We kept getting lost among all those huge stone buildings, those heaps just sitting there, radiating money, the calcification of empire. We tried to cross the Millennium Bridge, but it was being repaired. But the concert—that was the truly amazing part of the day."

We did eventually make it across the Thames, to the South Bank music halls. Ann's London is a city of the culture of the moment. So we took in plays, museums, movies, and lots of ethnic restaurants, the best of which were Persian, with their wonderful sesame flatbread. This was to be our first concert. We had grabbed at whatever tickets were available, without much thinking about the nature of the show.

"The chaabi Master," the poster reads. It shows a friendly-looking man smiling over a guitar. His name is El Hachemi Guerouabi.

We arrive early and take our seats. The auditorium begins filling up with handsome, dark-haired people. The elegant man next to me looks like a diplomat in his tailored suit and is accompanied by a woman wearing a ceremonial gown of midnight blue satin and ivory buttons. As people come down the aisle, he greets many of them. Only a few English faces can be seen in the crowd.

Five men stroll onto the stage, carrying drums, a banjo, a tambourine, a viola, and something that looks like the neck of a bass fiddle and is played with a bow. A man in his midsixties, with thick dark hair and glasses walks out, carrying a guitar. The crowd roars a rock-star welcome. He sits, adjusts the mike, hits a chord, and begins to sing.

How to describe another culture's music? To me, it sounds like the voice of the daily call to prayer fused with gypsy wildness. The strings create an unending ribbon of sound, and the words, so foreign to our ears, reduce to pure incantation. The songs are long and difficult to distinguish one from the other. It's a tormented music; I can't grasp its meaning, but I can feel its force.

Ann is bouncing up and down in her seat. "This is Arab pop without the techno," she says. "It's much more dissonant and austere than the stuff we get at TJU. I'm in heaven; my eyes keep filling up."

"Rarely has a music such at this been so strongly associated to Al Kasbah," I read in the flyer, "the famous rebellious place which inspired the classical film *la bataille d'Alger*."

Near the end of the second song, a curious thing happens.

The rhythm suddenly quickens, and the crowd gives out a whoop. At that moment, a few men jump up and begin dancing. Arms overhead, they point their fingers in the air and, with their feet more or less fixed in place, rotate their hips. The women clap with joy, and the men dance. A ululating sound rises up; it's the seated women, fluttering their tongues. A man on crutches struggles up from the front row, grasps the edge of the stage, and waves his arms with abandon, exhorting more and more men to their feet.

This happens again, song after song.

Ann and I begin to understand that we are taking part in a family affair: these people know each other, or know the same thing. This is their music.

It's a well-groomed crowd, in expensive wools and silks. A ticket for the evening starts at twenty dollars. These are Algerians. In exile. It's the professionals and the intellectuals who are forced to leave—or who elect to get out—if they can. They have come to England to make a life, or to save their lives.

But, of course, what they long for is Algeria. As Guerouabi plays what sounds like a national anthem, or the equivalent of "American the Beautiful," the auditorium stands as a body and cries out, "One, two, three—Algérie!"

Even more than New York, London is a city of many-colored faces. The world is here. But the pot has not melted, nor does it seems to have been asked to melt. London provides refuge without expecting assimilation. No one has asked these people the question our grandfathers were asked: "When are you going to become a citizen?" These are not immigrants but émigrés.

The response to the music is of a people who have not willingly chosen the West; what we see and hear on this night, alone together in the crowd, is a deep longing to go home. And I think I understand a little of what they feel, since every time I fly to Europe I think about somehow being stranded there and then admit to myself that I can think of nothing more painful than exile.

It's Thanksgiving morning. Ann is making Shaker lemon pie. Ruth is bringing by her contributions: a cherry pie and a cranberry salad. But Milton has a cold, and they won't be making the trip to Barney's. We walk out and wave to him through the car window.

Luke is playing techno and doing his sit-ups.

"Do you have that Tortoise CD?" Ann asks him.

"I have *a* Tortoise CD," he answers.

"Did you ever find your lost CDs? No—I know. They drained the pool at the orgy where you lost your wallet and found them at the bottom."

Luke gives a little laugh. "No—that was a different party, when I thought the CDs had disappeared. Actually, I found them in the apartment. There all the time."

While reading the paper, Ann says, "If they don't include women in these Afghan peace talks, they might as well forget it."

"Do you want to go?"

"Yes—I'll bake something and take it. So far, it's shaping up to be another botched guy thing."

The word "regret" comes up twice this weekend, once in a conversation with Meleesa and once in a conversation with Luke.

Luke and I are driving over to Dad's when he begins talking about his life in school. There was the 790 on the SAT Verbal exam. And there was dropping out of high school a few weeks before graduation. There was getting the GED and the admission to Bard, and there was leaving college after freshman year.

"I remember in eighth grade they put us in the front row so they could keep an eye on us," Luke says. "I used to take lots of mental health days, when I'd watch AMC. At some point it just seemed too easy, getting good grades. I look at people who went ahead and did it, and how they're set up now. And I think about regret. I guess it was a parent thing."

Given the fact that there is no one I find more interesting to talk to, and no one who has shown, in the past year, more personal growth, I find it hard to share in any feeling of regret.

Meleesa and I grab a moment alone in the living room and she begins talking about going to see *AI*. "It wasn't a very good movie, but somehow it got to me. You remember, at the end, he gets his wish to bring his mother back, for a day. This child who never really felt loved. I started crying then, and I kept crying. I was sobbing all the way out of the theater. 'What's wrong?' Larry kept asking. 'What's wrong?' Later on, I figured it out.

"I had always thought of Mom's life as a tragedy. She died so young—in her prime, really—and it was so sudden. One thing I learned this year, with Larry's mom, is that it's better to be able to say good-bye. And then there was all the confusion before and after she died, Dad's changing his life. I suppose I held it against him for a lot of years. It wasn't that I blamed him for Mom's death—I think you may have done that, a little. There was so much talk about it not being an accident, that Mom had somehow been ready to go. But if you believed that, then it was only natural to start looking for causes and explanations and to start drawing people into a plot.

"No, what I held against him was not paying attention—or being able to pay attention—to what was happening to me. I remember thinking, 'Please see me for who I am. I'm not your perfect little girl.'

"Anyway, after seeing the movie and falling apart over it, I realized that I had been loved. That what happened to Mom is beyond knowing but that she had loved me. And that the tragedy was my loss of that, not having missed it.

"So there has been regret, too, about the decision to break things off with Dad."

We set out for Barney's around three. It's another clear day in the driest fall I can remember. Forty days without rain. Dad rides with Larry, Meleesa, and Kate; they leave half an hour earlier. When Ann and Luke and I pull up at Barney's farmhouse, they are following behind us.

"Couldn't read the map," Larry says. "But we were heading back this way when we saw you zip by."

We're standing on top of a hill in Rappahannock County. Barney and Mary have twenty-five acres of pasture and twenty-five of woods. When they bought the place, in 1974, it had a tiny cabin and a four-room Virginia farmhouse. Next to the farmhouse they dug out a huge foundation, built a squash court, and over that positioned a huge, high-ceiling living-dining room supported by a fieldstone chimney. A few years back,

Barney added the "barn," as we call it, a four-story office-guesthouse complex topped by a cupola that replicates the one on the top of Davenport College that he rigged up with a stereo and an octagonal bed during our last year at Yale.

Inside are Barney and Mary, their sons, Patrick and Timothy, Barney's mother, Ricki, and his sister and brother-in-law and their two girls. We are seven, and they are nine. Two turkeys. Chestnut stuffing. Mashed potatoes and gravy. Sautéed Brussels sprouts. Braised fennel. Scalloped oysters. Cranberry relish. Six bottles of wine. Cracker pudding. Lemon, cherry, and pumpkin pie.

On the last Thanksgiving we had with my Mom, Libby and I were living in Oakland, in our first year of graduate school. We hemmed and hawed about whether we would fly to San Bernardino for the holiday. Dad insisted that we do and that we make it a surprise for Mom.

For twenty years she had been without a real washer-dryer; the family wash got done at a laundromat. That fall—it was 1970—Dad promised to buy her the two machines. Then he spirited us down from the north and picked us up at the airport. Just before we arrived at the house, he stopped the van and hid us inside two huge cardboard boxes. He drove home, parked, and brought Mom out of the house. She was exclaiming over the arrival of a washer and a dryer when we jumped out of the boxes.

The trouble with an accident is that it raises questions of responsibility that cannot be answered.

What one can do is to compose an evening in which being there together is enough.

At the end of dinner, after we've scattered for dessert, Barney calls us back to the table for a belated grace. I sit down between Larry and Dad. Everyone holds hands. Barney invites people to say things. "Dave, do you have anything?"

I haven't prepared anything to say. The silence before I speak is real; then I remember a morning exchange.

"Well, Ann and I were talking earlier about how comfortable we always feel when we come here. I don't know anywhere else where I feel such complete hospitality. So I wanted to thank you for this place and for all the hard work that makes it possible."

Someone uses the word "reunion," with a nod toward Meleesa and Dad.

Dad pauses and then says, in his usual sparkly way, "Everyone wants a miracle. This is a miracle. And I'm grateful." My forehead is dripping sweat, and I'm getting cramps in my hands.

"Yes," Meleesa says, "I've been at Barney and Mary's for lots of transitions in my life. Larry and I first visited about twenty years ago, on our way to New York. Then Kate and I were here for David and Ann's wedding. And now today. It's really wonderful to be sitting together. I want to thank you for having us here."

Then it's Barney's turn. He is not a man of many words and often falls asleep before the end of dinner. But he has a strong sense of occasion and of his responsibility toward the clan.

"It's been a hard fall," Barney says. "The events of September 11 have allowed us all to become aware of how much we have to be grateful for but also of those we have lost and who are not here to share this day with us. My father and Patrick and Timothy's grandfather, John. And James's wife and Dave and Meleesa's mother, Joy."

Joy. That was the name she took when we all joined the Group and changed our names.

Thirty years gone. She would have been seventy-seven this Monday. And the strange part—the terrible part—is that I cannot imagine what life would have been like if she had lived. The thought brings home to me, again and more achingly than ever, the scandal at the heart of things, which is not that we lose the people we love, as we all do and must, but that we get over losing them.

I do have one regret. After my mother was killed, it was agreed that she would be cremated. According to the belief system the family then held, the soul rises after death, waits a while, and then reenters existence to continue its evolution. So the fate of the body was for us not a central concern. No one gave any thought to a burial, and of the need for a spot to visit over the years where we could remember and pay our respects. I do regret not being able to do that.

The casket at the funeral was closed. In fact, the cremation may have occurred beforehand. When I asked after the ashes, I was told that they had been scattered from the air. The idea settled into my mind that the plane had done its work over the ocean. My mother's ashes then began their work of continually returning as they washed up at Santa Monica, and Huntington, and Oceanside. Hers was a spread-out death, a sudden vanishing in which, since none of us had been given the chance to say good-bye or to see the body, my mother passed not only into memory but into the very wind and water of the turning earth. This unlocatable and unending act of burial has become an experience I have learned to live with, accept, and even value over the years, since it is also one that insistently brings home the loss, and keeps it green.

The way home from Barney's takes us down the road that winds along the base of the Blue Ridge. Route 231, one of my favorite drives in all the world. And we are going back to it now—the world—that place the poet says has neither joy, nor love, nor light, nor certitude, nor peace, nor help for pain.

I do not believe him. Too many good things have come to us during this appalling fall to bear any grudge against whatever it is we mean when we say that word. *World*.

The sun on the watercourses; cattle grazing on the last sproutings of summer grass. Broomsedge pink in the fields. Old Rag Mountain bulges out from the range. Down the road, we will come to the "Ark of Saftey," with its hand-painted sign, a settlement where some believers live. Around Etlan, the apple orchards have begun a slow retreat, with more trees pulled up every year.

It is night, so I can see none of this. But I know how the land lies. Ann sleeps in the back seat; Luke rides beside me. We begin talking, a slow murmur in the dark. He likes to save up errands, like laundry, for when he comes to see us, and has big plans for tomorrow.

Epilogue

July 29, 2002

Back out of this now all too much for us, back in the maple double bed in the cottage at the Cape, feeling the sun burning through the built-in venetian blinds, we are awakened on the first morning of our month away by the whimpering of the dog. Ann goes out and then returns for her father's Second World War binoculars.

"Dave—Dave, come look," she yells from the top of the dune. "There are big fish all over the beach."

"Get a bucket and bring some home for dinner."

"They're bigger than that."

So I get up, throw on a T-shirt and trunks, and without coffee or even a splash of water in the face head outside.

And there, a quarter of a mile out, beached near the low tide, are whales.

I can't see any of this at first glance, just the circle of gawkers around a charcoal-colored pile. It's a Monday and a little after eight, so the beach isn't yet filled with people. Already it's a hazy, hot day, the sky the color of the land. Out ahead, Ann breaks into a run. She's wearing her green and white polka-dot one-piece and the Hugo Boss shirt I wore at our wedding.

They lie in huddles on the sand, each whale touching another one. I count thirty in one group before I stop; there must be at least ten more in the two smaller whale drifts nearby. People have begun covering the bodies with sheets and beach towels. "To prevent sunburn," someone says.

They lie forty yards from the tide line, now at its ebb. It will be at least four hours, I calculate, before the incoming tide reaches the first whale.

"Try to keep them wet," says a woman in an official-looking baseball cap. "And douse the paisley one, over there." We use what we have, mostly children's beach pails, in colors of yellow, purple, and orange. A line starts to form, and soon I am passing water hand-to-hand. Ann begins carrying water to the center of the pile; she steps lightly, hopscotching between the patches of exposed sand.

"Keep their tails wet," a voice instructs. "And don't dump the water—pour it, slowly. Otherwise you can send them into shock."

They are pilot whales. Some of the whales are as short as a sofa, others as long as limousines. They look utterly smooth, like the most perfect Michelin ever made. The skin is a rich, deep gray; the belly lightens toward white. Some lie on their sides, trapping their long, narrow flippers. Scars on the undersides; a ledger of pain. The noses are rounded like a cigar. I can see only two bodily openings, the blow-hole on the top of the head, which spews air every twenty seconds, and the anus, from which, on many of the bodies, a foamy liquid appears to be seeping. One or two of the animals thrash about, flipping their tails. The rest lie quietly on the sand.

The bureaucracy has arrived. Pickups from the Dennis Harbor Patrol dot the beach, and a backhoe scoops up a dead whale. It is pregnant, I am told. Reporting on the rescue, the *Cape Cod Times* will maintain that "pilot whales stick together no matter what."

The authorities begin trying to impose themselves. "We're taking volunteer names," a man with a clipboard announces, as they push us back away from the whales. For a few minutes the beach is clear of people while they corral us behind yellow police tape. We dutifully sign in and return to the whales. The attempt to manage the situation soon breaks down as people begin to overflow the line.

Ann will be quoted in the *Patriot Ledger* about rescue officials asking volunteers to back off. "I was miffed at first and cursed for about five minutes because we had been working all morning to keep the whales wet. They finally abandoned their bureaucratic instincts and allowed us to help." I doubt that Ann has ever used the word "miffed" in her life.

I shouldn't touch them, I think. I'll keep working the bucket brigade. But there are gaps in the line, so, despite the tape that cordons off the growing number of spectators, I run over to the crowd, grab two boys, and ask them to help.

Two very big men I've seen over at the Ponderosa rental cottage have begun ferrying a huge tub of water from the tide line to the largest pile of whales. They hold it by rope handles; the thing must weigh close to two hundred pounds. People dip their smaller sand pails into it and then fan out to water a whale. I can see Ann still working the middle of the pod, her shirt now tied around her waist. Most people have decided to focus on one animal, keeping it continually wet. I can't do this, I discover, and keep circling the pile, looking for dry skin. Someone has numbered the whales with a pink grease pencil.

"It's better doing this today than in twenty-degree weather," a man next to me says, and I realize that we are working alongside professional rescuers.

I am near a medium-size whale, emptying my bucket. Pieces of its skin have come off, like very thin black electrical tape. The whale's eye seems to stare at nothing. I look at its back and then put out my hand.

The body is utterly smooth and receives my touch, the flesh giving way ever so slightly. The whale feels solid and warm; it's like resting my hand on Norma's body if she had no hair. It seems possible to believe that the whale senses I am here to help.

It is one of those days—and are there more or fewer of them as I grow older?—on which it feels possible to believe again Robert Jordan's dying claim, that the world is a fine place and worth the fighting for.

Nearby an officious redhead in a bikini and baseball cap is talking to herself, too loudly. "We can't save any of them," she can be overheard to say. Then she tones it down. "If I save eight of them, I'll be lucky." It's clear that none of us will tolerate such talk, so she stops.

It turns out that beached pilot whales can die in a number of ways, if they are not sick to begin with. Sunstroke. Dehydration. Or their own weight, designed to remain always afloat, can crush their internal organs.

The Indians called pilot whales "blackfish." North of us on the Cape is a place called Blackfish Pond. Pilot whales have been beaching themselves on Cape Cod in numbers large and small for two hundred years.

The morning passes in a labor of dipping and pouring. It's past noon now; I can tell by the angry color of Ann's exposed back. As the tide begins to come in—it's now only ten feet from the outermost pile—she joins me there. "I like cleaning their faces, as much as anything," Ann says. We throw ourselves in the rising water and then go back to work.

"Try to get their bodies right side up and pointed out to sea," someone says. "And try to work the flippers free."

And now the sheets we have draped over the whales come in handy. As the tide begins to lift our whale, we work the sheet under its belly and deploy it as a sling. A man on each end of the sheet lifts the whale's head while four of us steady its body. The water has risen to my waist. With one arm over the whale's back and another under its belly, I brace my feet in the sand and lean against the incoming tide. I am all over the whale.

Most of the whales are now afloat. A few break free, flipping their tails as they go, and move offshore. They wait there. Soon the entire pod is cavorting thirty yards out. Then they point their noses at us and swim toward land.

"Beat the water—make lots of noise!" So we make a conga line, two hundred strong, and scare the whales back out to sea. They circle for a few minutes and then swim north, toward Provincetown.

Fifty-five whales have come ashore at Dennis on this day, and only eleven have died.

Exhausted, Ann and I walk back to the cottage. Inside, I move to the stove and put the kettle on. I don't recall being this hungry.

"How will we go back to our lives after this?" Ann asks, over our coffee and eggs.

I'm not feeling ready for a moment of reflection and murmur something about things taking a while to sink in. Then I think of something to say.

"We've survived, but we haven't escaped. Found

again. Of all places. Isn't that what it feels like? Found again."

She senses my desire not to continue, and we finish our breakfast in silence. In this way, we begin our vacation together.

The next morning, the pod goes aground south of Wellfleet, in the mud flats at Bog Creek. Rescuers coax them out to sea, but the whales beach themselves again. Fourteen whales die, and thirty-one have to be euthanized.

Why do they go aground?

Pilot whales direct themselves by way of magnetic forces. An anomaly in the magnetic field near Wellfleet may have left them disoriented. Or perhaps an unusually high tide produced by a full moon lured them into shallow water. Or they may have been chasing squid. Or a sick or pregnant animal led the others onto the beach. The fact is, no one knows much about why pilot whales end up so often on land.

When Solon's son died, he went about weeping in the streets. Solon, the wise man. Someone asked him, "Solon, why do you weep, when it avails nothing?" And Solon answered, "*Because* it avails nothing."

"I saw a lot of people trying to release them from their heaviness," Ann later said, about the day with the whales. That's true, I thought, that's true. I saw that too.